I Am What I Ate...

and I'm frightened!!!

HarperEntertainment
An Imprint of HarperCollins*Publishers*

I Am What I Ate...
and I'm frightened!!!

**And Other Digressions
from the Doctor of Comedy**

BILL COSBY

With original illustrations by George Booth

HarperCollins books may be purchased for educational, business, or sales promotional use. For information please write: Special Markets Department, HarperCollins Publishers Inc., 10 East 53rd Street, New York, NY 10022.

FIRST EDITION

Designed by Nancy B. Field

Printed on acid-free paper

Library of Congress Cataloging-in-Publication Data
  Cosby, Bill, 1937–
    I am what I ate . . . and I'm frightened!!! : and other digressions from the doctor of comedy / by Bill Cosby.— 1st ed.
     p. cm.
  ISBN 0-06-054573-9 (hardcover)
    1. Cosby, Bill, 1937– 2. Comedians—United States—Biography. I Title.

PN2287.C632A3 2003
792.7'028'092—dc21
[B]   2003051097

03 04 05 06 07 ❖/RRD 10 9 8 7 6 5 4 3 2 1

To Camille,

who has worked very hard to make all this a happy ending

Contents

Contents

Introduction

When I turned sixty-five, I immediately set two goals for myself.

> *1.* Write a book about a healthy lifestyle. (And who better than I, someone who never had one.)

> *2.* Apply for my Social Security check.

I applied for a Social Security check at sixty-five years old. I'm not sure, but I understand there are people who applied at age sixty-two. Anyway, I applied at age sixty-five. And I really and truly suspect that my wife didn't want me to have these checks. That's because getting a Social Security check would mean I would have an income that would go past her. You see, my wife controls, she manages, whatever, all the money. So I have no idea what the things she buys cost. Whenever I ask my wife what something costs she gets amnesia, even though she might be holding the very thing in her hand—the sweater, the jumpsuit, the shoes. Something could be right there in her hand, something she just bought, with the tags still hanging from it that she will have to cut off before she goes out in public. And I say to her:

"How much was that?"

And it's almost like she blames me—this arrogant voice saying:

"I don't know what it costs!"

And the sound of her voice makes me feel it was my fault for even asking. So then I said:

"Can you give me a ballpark?"

And she said:

"I don't play sports."

Well, I applied for this check. And I'm very proud I am applying for this check, because I have been working—I have worked—every year, 365 days every year. And out of that I have paid Social Security. Therefore, I am looking forward to this check. It will be a sign of independence. Not that I would run away from my wife and family—I wouldn't do that. It's not that I want to run away from these people. The children are out of the house for as long as they want to stay out. Their mother welcomes them back. I call them squatters. One of them has deliberately gone out and had a child to send ahead of her. Because who wants to reject a child. She comes behind the child. But I don't trust the child either. The apple doesn't fall far from the tree, and because I brought up half of the kid's parents I know the kid's behavior can't be far from the mother's. So I don't trust this kid either.

But anyway, I don't mean to drift, it's just that I want you to know that I was feeling that this check was going to be a sign of my independence. In other words, without my going to work, without my going anywhere, a check comes to the address where I want it to come and it comes in *my* name. And no one can get a piece of this check like all the other checks I get. No, *this* check I can cash and do whatever I want to do with it. So if I want to, and I'm not saying

I will do this, but if I want to I can use the money to buy hoagies or halfsmokes or pizza or cake or anything else my wife says I shouldn't eat. And the beauty of it is that she doesn't have to know I'm buying these things. I won't have to go to my wife and say: "May I have a check for . . ." Not that my wife says, "Well, why do you want the money?" No, she doesn't say that. But it's just the feeling, having been married for thirty-nine years, it's just the feeling that *something* is mine.

When one uses the word *bureaucracy* as a negative term, one thinks of a huge building somewhere with a lot of windows, and the building, even in the daytime, seems to just have a negative grayish feeling about it. And inside there are people moving slowly, saying to one another: "I don't know where it is." Everybody walking around saying to one another: "I don't know where it is." Thousands of people in the building walking around different machines with papers spewing out onto the floor. And the trash cans are full. Paper airplanes flying around the cubicles and the chanting of "I don't know. I'm not doing that. You'll have to call someone else."

When one thinks of bureaucracy, one thinks of

a dollar actually being worth three cents. Blockage. People being told something will be there, but it isn't there. Bureaucracy. Being put on hold with no music, no sound. Just you and your ear and the phone. And you can make your own sound by rubbing the phone against your ear.

But bureaucracy can even happen in your own home. You can say:

"Has anybody seen my car?"

And they say:

"We don't know where it is. Somebody may have taken it."

And you say:

"Well, who authorized somebody to take my car?"

And they say:

"Well, I don't know."

And if you ask:

"Who's on my phone?"

They say:

"Well, you weren't here so somebody used it."

Bureaucracy. It's everywhere. Especially at the Social Security office. Right away I was told that I needed my birth certificate, which I didn't have. So my in-house bureaucracy sprang into action.

"Do you remember the hospital where you were born?" the head in-house bureaucratic person asked.

I told the head in-house bureaucratic person which hospital and added that I was born on July 12, 1937.

Anyway, I had to send off somewhere to get my birth certificate. While I was waiting for the birth certificate to arrive, the question I began to ask myself is the following:

Why did I have to prove I was born?

The only other time anyone asked me to prove I was born was when I applied for a driver's license. And I wasn't that old then. I was sixteen. When a person is sixteen, it's understandable that they ask for proof the person exists. After all, at that point, the sixteen-year-old person hasn't done very much in the real world to show he was born. He's living in the house with the only two people he owes money. There are no documents that indicate he has done anything. Plus, nobody really wants a sixteen-year-old to have a driver's license. A sixteen-year-old doesn't have a job. He doesn't even have a car. So, naturally, the Motor Vehicles people make a sixteen-year-old prove he was born.

Anyway, a sixteen-year-old doesn't mind if someone asks him to prove he was born. But I'm sixty-five! I have been on this earth for sixty-five years, and yet they want me to prove I was born! I'm closer to checking out than being born!

When I joined the navy—and I was joining to put my life on the line for my country—I don't recall someone saying: "You must bring your birth certificate." I think all I had to show was a driver's license to prove I had in fact driven in the United States. Which, of course, should be enough, since you need to show your birth certificate in order to get a driver's license in the first place.

When I applied for a credit card, for permission to run up a bill on a platinum card and then run away, they never asked me if I was born. They never asked for proof of being born.

When I received the Presidential Medal of Freedom last year, they didn't ask: "Were you born?" They called me and said we think you're this and that. But nobody asked: "Were you born?"

But to receive this money that I loaned the government so they could play with it until I reached this age and then give me some of my money back, only for this do I have to prove that I was born. I have to send away to get a copy of my birth certificate to give to the government to prove to the government I exist. And where do I send away to get this birth certificate? The government. Yes. They already *have* my birth certificate. But now I need to ask the government to give me a copy of my birth certificate so I can give it back to them.

My birth certificate finally came in the mail. Someone in my home made a copy of it and all the forms were filled out and I sent the paperwork to the Social Security office in Washington, D.C. And then I waited. Six months went by. Nothing. I checked the mail every day. Nothing. I guess they think that old people have nothing better to do than sit and wait. But after six months I was tired of waiting.

So one day I decided that maybe it would be better if I applied for my Social Security check in the small Social Security office in a nearby small town. So I asked the person who is the head of the small bureaucracy in my house (and I'm not saying who that person is) about the possibility of applying for my check in the small town down the road. And this person said:

"You need your birth certificate. They will not give you the money if you don't have the birth certificate."

So now I'm back to the birth certificate again. So I asked the head bureaucrat in my house:

"Well, we sent for it and it came in the mail. So, where is my birth certificate?"

And this person said:

"It's where it belongs."

And I said:

"Where is that?"

And the person began to sound a little irritated. But at least this is my in-house bureaucracy—they don't put you on hold. That's the only good thing. But soon you have the feeling that you're going to be yelled at and there's going to be an argument.

So the person said look in this and look in that, which we did, and we found the birth certificate. Another person (not the head bureaucratic person) is now going to go to town with my birth certificate, and then I'm going to do the interview over the phone while the person in town at the small Social Security office is showing my birth certificate to the Social Security people and then I will have my money.

As the person with my birth certificate is leaving, the head bureaucratic person says:

"Don't do that."

"Do what?" I said.

And the head bureaucratic person of my house said:

"Don't have someone go to town with that and start that because we don't know what has been started."

"I don't understand what you mean 'what's been started,'" I replied. "It's been since July."

"People have been working on this thing for you," barked the head bureaucratic person of my house. "And we don't know what they've done. I've got to call sometime today and find out what they have done and what's started."

"What could have been started?" I protested.

The in-house bureaucratic person started to raise the voice.

"I'm telling you," said the in-house bureaucratic person, "don't go to town."

"But it makes no sense," I pointed out. "They've had my papers—"

The in-house bureaucratic person looked at me and said:

"I don't want to talk about it."

So I called back the person who was going to town with my birth certificate, and an idea came to me.

"I would like to talk to the in-town bureaucratic person," I said. "How large is the office?"

"It's very, very small," the person said. "Just two people sitting around when I went there."

So I said: "Dial them. I just want to talk to them and ask them some questions. Maybe they will interview me and then say well yes, you can come in and get your check. That way I can go over the head of the head in-house bureaucratic person."

It's not making any sense to me because the in-house bureaucratic people have had this for six months. And this in my house! These are people who work for me in my own bureaucracy.

So I'm waiting and waiting and waiting for the in-house bureaucratic person to buzz me and put the in-town bureaucratic people on the phone. As will happen, people forget to get back to you and tell you what happened and an hour passed and I buzzed the intercom around the house looking for the in-house bureaucratic person who was supposed to get in touch with the in-town bureaucratic people. So finally I saw an in-house bureaucratic person walking around the property and I said have you seen this other in-house bureaucratic person. And the in-house bureaucratic person said:

"Yes. He had to run an errand for somebody, but he said to tell you he would be back."

And I said:

"How long have you known this?"

And this person said:

"About forty minutes. But I've been busy doing something over here."

So I went back in the house trying to readjust my ego on exactly what position I am, in this bureaucracy. The in-house bureaucratic person came back and I went to that person and I said:

"Did you get in touch with the in-town bureaucratic people?"

And he said:

"No, they put me on hold and nobody's answering now."

"But it's a very small office," I said.

And he said: "Yes."

And then he walked away.

So that's where I am now. Bureaucratically held in limbo. In Washington, D.C. In the small town. And even in my own house.

But I digress.

I was talking about writing a book. And the book I had decided to write was about health. Now, the thing you do to check your health is go to the doctor for a physical. So that's the first thing I did. I went to the doctor. And I went through the usual. He did the chest X ray. Took some blood. That kind of thing. And then the doctor came into the examination room and said:

"Well, Mr. Cosby, your heart is fine. EKG was okay."

I smiled.

"Your lungs are fine. Chest X ray was negative."

I smiled again.

"Overall, you seem to be in pretty good shape."

"Thank you, Doctor."

"*But* . . . ," the doctor said.

And the word *but* just sent shock waves through my body. But *what*? You're in good shape but you're dying? But what?

"Your cholesterol is four hundred and seventy," the doctor continued. "And the good versus the bad is not good at all. As a matter of fact, you have no good."

My body relaxed. That's all? High cholesterol? I smiled and said:

"Thank you, Doctor."

"Well," the doctor said with a frown, "you don't seem to be upset by this, Mr. Cosby."

"No, I'm not, Doctor."

"Why?"

"Well, my cholesterol is supposed to be that high. I eat pies. Cakes. Like I have always said, it's supposed to be high when you eat like I eat."

The doctor looked at me and asked:

"Have you had any trouble?"

Suddenly I was concerned again.

"Trouble? What trouble?"

"Have you had any trouble?"

"Trouble? Where?"

"Well," the doctor said, "with cholesterol as high as yours, I think we better check the carotid artery. There could be some blockage."

Now generally, you can wish things away. But carotid artery! Blockage! These are words one doesn't want to hear in the same sentence. Blockage in the carotid artery is not something you can wish away. And there's nothing you can take that will make it go away. In other words, unlike a car with a clogged motor, there is no oil treatment for the blood where you take it and then it goes up and flushes out your carotid artery. There is no carotid flush-out. I mean that blockage is there. It's plaque. And there is no carotid artery floss. Not even if you're a grand master of yoga. You can't put a string in your nose and floss. Because there's the danger that if these particles break loose, they could go up to your brain and turn the lights out and you'll be in the permanent horizontal parade rest. So this stuff, this plaque, is stuck. And I thought to myself, Oh my God! I am what I ate.

And I'm frightened.

I Am What I Ate

All those years. The youthful heart. The carefree, reckless taste buds. You see, to saturate or unsaturate depends on one's taste. And my taste buds have gotten me into more trouble. And you don't want to think about what all those things are doing to your body. How many pieces of scrapple? How many hot dogs? How many pieces of bacon? All those hoagies. All those steak sandwiches. Ice cream. Man! I'm terrified. I'm in trouble. Because I suddenly realize that I *am* what I ate, and I'm frightened.

All that butter. And some of it was just casual. *Casual.* Just sitting there. The butter was there. And the bread was there. So why not? Bread. With butter. It was casual. No harm. But there is no such thing as casual because it's on the side of my neck now.

Those mornings in the south of France at the Hôtel du Cap. After walking six miles. And I would buzz the room service waiter and he would come to the room and say:

"Round up the usual suspects, sir?"

Meaning four croissants. (Made in France, I'm telling you, which is like having a biscuit in Atlanta.) And a large cup of espresso with steamed milk. Along with the usual suspects comes butter. We all know that in each croissant there's at least a quarter pound of butter. Nonetheless, I would take a patty and spread it on the croissant and then empty out two little things of blueberry jam and one thing of marmalade and mix them together and put it on top of the croissant. I would bite into it, sip on that coffee, and that mixture was fantastic.

But now the doctor is telling me I could have blockage in my carotid artery. The plaque. And it keeps on plaquing. And I thought to myself: Time is going by and this stuff is just plaquing up.

So the doctor sent me to a place where they put

these things on my chest and I got on the treadmill and I started walking. And the treadmill increased every three minutes and after I reached 150 rpm of my heart per second, they yanked me off and they walked with me and I felt like somebody who'd been thrown out of a bar or something. Then they put me horizontal and they started to put instruments on the side of my neck, checking my carotid artery. And I heard these squishing sounds. When all the testing was over, I went back to the doctor and he looked at me and he said:

"You have a thirty percent blockage in your carotid artery."

That was not good news. And I was mad at myself. And so I said to myself: *You started out with a clean carotid. Fantastic! Now look what you've done!*

Believe it or not, even though my body was shaking and my brain was reeling, my mouth was watering. Which proves how stupid my taste buds really are. So I told my mouth: *You will never have these things you like again. Water all you want, but you've had your day.*

Blockage! Thirty percent blockage and more to come. Scrapple. One of the great tastes of all time.

But if you want to squeeze it after you cook it, or just put it on a piece of paper, you'll be able to see your own carotid artery. I've seen a simple slice of scrapple cooked to a dark brown—then placed on a piece of paper towel—and the scrapple killed the paper towel. The grease clotted the paper towel. Turned it into a sheet of saturated carotid artery blocking glop.

I am what I ate, and it frightens me.

It's not a matter of one's left arm going numb, it's a matter of knowing deep down inside while we're running a machine on bad fuel that things eventually are going to happen to that machine. It's going to break down.

Thirty percent blockage! I can't afford to go with my taste buds anymore. I know it sounds pitiful. But when does one realize that the last dance was in fact the last dance and you don't have to dance anymore. That you have to tell the taste buds that was it. That the taste buds have to know, along with the memory, that if you want to live longer, just stop it. It's not as easy as one thinks. Because along with it comes the smell. So you begin to smell things, see them, your mouth waters. But you have to move on.

By the way, leave the people alone who are eating. There's no need for you to go from table to table and say: You know, you're blocking your carotid artery. There's no sense in getting angry when you see somebody older than you still eating it and they're okay. Their body is not the same as yours. And who knows? Maybe that person eating all those things might have the same percent blockage or worse. And they just said: "I don't care."

Please don't try to push them and hope they fall out of the chair so you can say: "That's the carotid."

Blockage! Oh, my goodness. Popcorn. With butter. Oh my goodness. Pancakes. With butter. And then the same meal would slide gracefully to eggs over easy between the pancakes. Bacon. And sausage. Forget the turkey bacon. Just get some good old-fashioned pork sausage. Espresso with steamed milk. Blueberry jam on the side to cover up the holes left by the syrup, places that the syrup missed. Never been big on milk shakes, but I have had my share. Pies and cakes. Lard.

I am what I ate, and I'm frightened.

And I became even more frightened when I did

some research on the carotid artery. I went to the Internet and got on to the home page of the American Heart Association. There was an article that listed as coauthors Costas Tsioufis, M.D.; Skevos Sideris, M.D.; Christodoulos Stefanadis, M.D.; and Pavlos Toutouzas, M.D. So with all those doctors helping to write the article I thought what they had to say would probably be true. The headline on the article said:

CLOGGED NECK ARTERY MAY WARN OF HEART ATTACK AS WELL AS STROKE

Heart attack? Stroke? What have I done to myself? The article started out:

Extensive fatty deposits in the carotid arteries, the blood vessels in the neck that supply blood and oxygen to the brain, may be a marker for coronary artery disease, according to a study in this month's *Stroke: Journal of the American Heart Association.*

The vessel that supplies blood and oxygen to my brain is 30 percent blocked!

Then there was a part in that article that said:

> Among the 54 patients who had both severe heart
> disease and impaired pumping power—a major
> predictor of heart attack—46.3 percent also had
> severe atherosclerosis in the carotid arteries.

Impaired pumping power. That's what I had.
What does that mean? Is that like a car with a broken fuel pump? Am I operating at only 70 percent
power? Can I make it up a hill?

The article also talked about a study by a doctor named Ioannis Kallikazaros, M.D., associate
director in cardiology at Hippokration Hospital in
Athens, Greece. (In case you're wondering, the
study took place in Greece.) Anyway, Dr.
Kallikazaros put blocked people into categories,
depending on their blockage.

> Kallikazaros and his colleagues assigned
> patients to one of five groups categorizing the
> severity of the atherosclerosis in both their
> carotid and coronary arteries.

> The carotid artery classifications were: (1) no
> sign of plaque; (2) 2 to 15 percent artery

obstruction; (3) 16 to 49 percent artery obstruction; (4) 50 to 79 percent artery obstruction; and (5) 80 to 100 percent artery obstruction.

There I was! In group three—sixteen to forty-nine percent blocked!

I decided that I felt badly. I didn't like those numbers. The numbers were frightening—although I had a feeling that my cholesterol was high—when a doctor says high cholesterol and you're sixty-five, it puts you in a very stressful position. Plus, I had no idea that I had 30 percent blockage in my carotid artery. Now I know I'm a walking time bomb. My veins, my arteries, even my liver capillaries, are ready to be clogged and I'll explode and die. And I immediately knew what my mantra was going to be.

I'll never go back to the doctor again.

2

If I Don't Go to the Doctor, I Don't Have It

So that's what I was thinking when I left the doctor's office. I don't want to see him anymore. Because I know that had I not gone to him, my cholesterol would have never been as dangerous as it is. I was doing just fine before that doctor said to me that it was dangerous. And my carotid artery would not have a blockage. I knew what I was eating and I knew what I was doing and I knew when to cut off. I was looking for the warning signs. But he warned me before the signs came.

I remember that while eating his fourteenth crab cake Uncle Ernie Fletcher said to me:

"Doctors will spoil a dying man's habit."

And Uncle Ernie had to have been around 42 when he said it. And he lived to be 116. Now that just shows you what doctors know about crabs and crab cakes. Crab cakes are supposed to be very dangerous if they are fried in trans fats. Of course, by the time they're fried and you put the filling in the crab cake, you may have done some horrible things. This is what doctors say.

Most doctors joined the medical profession to save lives. And then they met the patients. And this is when things went bad. Because they found that the patients really were not as interested in saving their lives as the doctors were. They found that the patients come to them too late. Many of them come and don't want to hear what the cure is. They only want to know how they can keep living like they're living and not die when the doctor's only answer is: You can't. And so if you don't go to the doctor, then you don't have it and you're not going to have to listen to the doctor tell you you're going to get it.

If I seem to be rambling it's because these were my thoughts in trying to get myself back into some sort of settled position after being knocked off balance.

Your heart is fine, he said. Lungs are fine. You have the body of a forty-seven-year-old man, and I'm sixty-five. But then he dropped the number on me. He didn't have to do that. If I had this kind of body, why is he bringing me down with something called cholesterol?

So clearly, I don't want to go back to see this man, this doctor, or any other doctor again. Because it is my philosophy that if you don't go to the doctor, you don't have it. If the doctor doesn't see you, you don't have it. The only time you should go to a doctor is when you have it. By that time, it's too late. But that's okay because nobody frightened you.

I remember Doctor Bowles watching me as I lit up a cigar. He didn't back off, he didn't run away, he just sat there at the table and very calmly said to me:

"How long have you been smoking?"

"Forty years."

Doctor Bowles shook his head and said: "Why would you do something that is going to kill you in about sixty years?"

And I thought to myself: I know what he's trying to do and I appreciate what he's saying. Okay.

Sometimes people try to help you, sometimes people try to talk to you, and you still don't understand it. So I've been talking to my wife about what it is that might help people understand. Well, my wife and I agreed that sometimes people—doctors especially— miss the significance of putting together a tangible group of words that hits the human being right between the eyes so that they put the cigarette down and they never puff again. And they ask God's forgiveness and they hope it isn't too late for themselves.

For example, after the doctor hit me with this number, I asked him a question about high cholesterol.

"What do you want me to do?"

He told me I had to change my diet. And so I asked:

"What can I eat, Doctor? Let's be realistic. I *can't,* and I don't want to go for the *rest* of my life on just boiled cauliflower and boiled zucchini."

The doctor looked at me and said:

"Well, we *do* want you to eat various fresh vegetables. We want you to stay away from the fried group of vegetables. We want you to stay away from egg yolks. We want you to stay away from dairy products like butter."

He started naming things and most things on the list were man-made. Pizza. Hot dogs. Scrapple. Bacon. Sausage. Cheese. Cheese. Cheese. Soft cheese. Hard cheese. Soft cheese. Cheese. Chocolate. Milk. Ice cream. Things that I love. And I sat there and I started to weep. My mouth was making me weep because it was saying you're never going to let me taste those wonderful things again. And then my mouth began to say that the doctor is not a good person. The doctor doesn't want us to live. The doctor just wants us to walk around with no hope at all. Why, there are days when we live for pizza. There are days that would have been unbearably boring had it not been for hot dogs with chili sauce. There are days that would have been just a waste of a living person's time had it not been for a hot fudge sundae. Yet, here I am looking at this doctor from hell who is telling me I don't need taste buds in order to live. I might as well get a suit made from bull skin and stay out on the meadow. Put it on and just stay out on the meadow, wandering around eating grass. Blowing dirt off of four-leaf clovers.

But it is for the mouth that I must eat and live

on. This is what I want to tell myself. A croissant! For the mouth. Double butter, double saturated. Eat it and clot. And the mouth will say: Thank you. Meanwhile, one of the ventricles, like a bad downtown area in an urban city, will be closing down. Shut down because of saturates.

On the way to the airport in a car, as we go down the street, I see the fast-food restaurants on the left and the right side. I hate these restaurants. I hate them because I can't eat there anymore. And I'm beginning to look at the people coming out of these fast-food restaurants and some of these people look very large. But they're still up and walking around. And I'm thinking that there's a lot I could still lay on myself. I'm looking at a woman who must weigh 270 pounds. I weigh 180, and I want to know why my doctor said I can't have it and her doctor said she could continue to go in there and get some fries. I want to know. And now I'm a very, very angry person. And I see a man coming out of a chicken place and he's got a whole chicken in his hands and he's eating it. And he must weigh at least 350 pounds and *he's not dead yet!* So why do I have to watch myself? If I can go to 350 and still walk around eating a chicken, what the hell is wrong with this doctor who told me I'd gone far enough? Sometimes these people just don't want me to have fun.

Anyway, I left the doctor's office and got in a car to go to the airport. So here I am, sitting in a car riding to the airport looking at a pamphlet that says I can have boiled things. No cholesterol there in the boiled things. I can have fish. Boiled. Chicken, poached. (I don't know the difference.) I can put a lot of lemon on everything. It appears that's the closest I'm going to get to flavoring. Lemon and lime. No potato—the potato is dead. And now here's this pamphlet telling me that I can't satisfy my taste buds anymore. What a cruel, cruel thing.

Had I some warning, I think I would not feel as badly. Had I some warning, I know that the night before when I had that hot fudge sundae with the almonds on it, I would've tasted the hot fudge sundae in a different way. I would've left it in my mouth a little longer, I would have wallowed it around a little slower. I think I would have made more noises, more soft noises. Note: The almonds were there for health reasons, which I get no credit for. See, I did say to the doctor: "Yeah, it's four hundred and seventy. But what about the almonds I had last night? Is there no credit for that?" And he said I was out of line for asking that question.

And I think a good pizza with the sausage and the pepperoni and the double cheese—the way I love it—is just wonderful. You pull a slice and then a second slice and put one slice on top of the other and just bite down, close your eyes, and try not to let saturated grease run down the corner of your mouth.

I would have tasted pizza more if I had known that one day I could never eat pizza again. As it is, I think I just gobbled every slice. I should have chewed longer and I should have eaten the crust.

And if only I could live last night over again when I had that hot fudge sundae. I squandered last night. And I squandered yesterday afternoon when I had that pepperoni double cheese pizza. And I knew—I'm so angry with myself—I *knew* when I ate that pizza I was going to have blood tests. But I felt that if I ate it at three, I could throw it off.

So I arrived at the airport and got on the plane. The flight attendant came by with peanuts. And I looked at my pamphlet. Oddly enough, the peanuts were okay, but the salt on the peanuts was no good. And so I took the bag of peanuts and I asked for a glass of water. And I poured the peanuts in a glass of water. Shook them up. (The fellow sitting next to me asked the flight attendant to move him to another seat.)

It was an hour-and-forty-minute flight back. I let the peanuts soak, moved them around, and then took a teaspoon and put them on a plate. And I gave the water to the flight attendant. I don't think all the salt was gone because I could still taste some, but I *did* think I had done a wonderful thing. And I asked the flight attendant for a fresh glass of water in order to wash down the peanuts. As the flight attendant walked away, the thought entered my mind that water and peanuts were something for a prisoner.

"Here's your water and peanuts and you will never escape from Devil's Island again!!!"

The plane landed and I walked into the airport and down the corridor past all the fast-food places. I smelled coffee. I smelled potato chips. *Through the bag.* And I pretended I wanted to buy a magazine, but I was actually smelling some of the pastry.

So there I was. Pitiful. A finished person. But then, all of a sudden, I remembered something the doctor had said. And it gave me hope. A will to go on. The doctor had said that I could have pizza and cheese and saturates "once in a while." I smiled. I sighed. And I said to myself: Once in a while!

Once in
a While

And now I am remembering it very clearly. The doctor said "once in a while." In fact, now I recall exactly what he said as I sat there glumly looking forward to a life of nothing. He said:

"Nobody's saying you have to eat like this every day. You can have ice cream once in a while."

And my eyes lit up when he said that. Once in a while! Oh, this is wonderful! Once in a while! But let me tell you the problem with once in a while. The problem with once in a while is amnesia. Because once in a while can only be as long as you remember the *once*. When did I last eat it? I don't remember.

Has it been long enough to have it again? I think it has. Henceforth, here's the discrepancy with once in a while. And certainly we all forget and we forget on purpose. When did you have that last doughnut? I don't remember. Has it been long enough? Well, it's certainly been a while. But *has* it? Why can't a doctor simply look at us and say: Let me tell you how long "a while" is? You name something that's on that list that you cannot eat. Four slices of pizza, for example, with meatballs, sausage, and pepperoni, and double cheese. And then the doctor tells you how long you must wait before you can have it again.

How long "once in a while" is bothered me all the way home. So I just dropped my bags in the hall and went right back out to a doctor I know down the street from my house. And I asked him:

"Doctor. If I can have four slices of pizza, with meatballs, sausage, and pepperoni, and double cheese once in a while, how long is once in a while?"

The doctor picked up his antihuman handheld computer and typed for a long time. Clickety-click-click-click. Then he looked up and said:

"In reality, if you eat four large slices of a large pizza, with meatballs, double cheese, sausage, and pepperoni—and you even eat the crust—*once in a while* . . ."

The doctor looked down at the little antihuman computer, then looked up at me and said:

"For you to throw that off and get rid of it? Three months."

I gasped. Three months!

"Doctor," I said. "In other words, you're telling me that if I eat four slices of pizza, with meatballs, sausage, and pepperoni, and double cheese, then I have to go *three months* before I can have it again?"

"Yes."

"Okay. So. Is there a quicker way?"

"Yes."

"What?"

"Eat just half of it."

I mulled that over for a moment. Okay. I can do that. I can eat just *two* slices of pizza, with meatballs, sausage, and pepperoni, and double cheese and my mouth will still be happy.

"Okay, Doctor," I said. "If I eat half of something, then how long?"

"Three months."

I frowned and said, "I don't understand."

"Well," the doctor explained, "if you consume four slices, then your cholesterol is going to go up. But if you just eat half, it'll be just half as high as it was. But it will still take three months for the saturated fat to work its way out of your system."

"Oh, I understand," I groused. "If I don't eat it at all, then the three months just becomes a period of time I would have to myself with great cholesterol. So let me get this straight. If I don't eat anything like that for three months, what will my cholesterol be?"

"Your cholesterol will be very, very low."

"And suppose, Doctor, I exercise."

"Well, that depends on the exercise."

"I think I can do that," I lied. "I think I can exercise and not eat anything."

So when is once in a while? Well, it's clear—the doctor made it clear—that I should never have asked that question. Because now I know that once in a while is three months. And now I have to figure out how to enjoy life once in a while. Because when you're dead you can eat anything you want.

So I went home and opened the refrigerator and . . . my God! It was all there. And all these things were beautiful. Chocolate cake! Cheese! Ham! Seven slices of leftover pizza. A piece of pie. They were there wrapped. Like little presents for my mouth.

I went to the bread bin and there they were! My friends. My friends from a long time ago. Yesterday. Bagels. Doughnuts. Cookies. And they were there and they were waiting for me. Waiting for my hands to reach in and grab them and welcome them. And my taste buds were thanking me in advance for all kinds of wonderful things.

It was then that I decided to find out the truth about myself. Could I really and truly walk away from these things and only have them once in a while? And the answer was yes. And to prove to myself that I could in fact walk away anytime I wanted to, I made myself a sandwich. I took a bagel, cut it in half, pulled out the middle—the dough in there, I pulled it out. And then I toasted it. And then I added ham, cheese, and roast beef, two pickles and mustard. And I wrapped it in a paper towel and I poured a glass of orange juice for healthful reasons. And I put the sandwich on a plate and I said: "This is the enemy I'm looking at. And I will stare at it. And I will prove that I am bigger than this."

I kept telling myself I didn't want the sandwich,

didn't *need* the sandwich. But I was beginning to feel light-headed because I hadn't eaten anything except those peanuts, and now I was just staring at a sandwich. So I went back in the kitchen and I looked in the vegetable bin. Mrs. Cosby's area. And I saw some broccoli. So I pulled a piece off and ate it raw. And my stomach almost exploded. It said it needed it cooked. So I pulled some out and put it in the water—after washing it I put it in the water—and I found a piece of fish in Mrs. Cosby's bin: cod. And I thought: This is good. Cod is a good fish. As a matter of fact, it's a good fish to have because I remember as a child having to take a teaspoon of cod liver oil. And I was wondering if there was enough oil in the cod itself to help me.

And so I boiled the two together—the cod held up—and I put them on my plate and I took a knife and fork and the napkin and the glass of orange juice. I put the sandwich in the refrigerator. And I went upstairs to my office to eat a piece of boiled broccoli and boiled cod. Actually, it didn't taste bad. The taste buds kind of liked it, but I think mostly my body liked it. It said: Gee whiz! This is kind of nice and it tasted delicious. Thank you so much. In other words, my body was desperate.

I chewed this food a long time. And the reason I chewed it a long time was because of the taste. Boiled broccoli has a taste that makes you chew it a long time. Not that it tastes beautiful, it's just that you don't want to swallow it. You just keep chewing it. And the cod mixed with it made for a wonderful flavor, but I wasn't hungry. And I didn't have gas. But I knew I was going to be hungry later because there was something missing from the diet. Salt. There was no salt there and everything was flat. But I had been good. And for this, I applauded myself. I have, in fact, been good.

My daughter stopped by the house for dinner. She had fried chicken, mashed potatoes, corn bread, collard greens, and ham hocks. So I explained to her about cholesterol and the concept of once in a while. Then I asked her why she was eating all those things that were bad for her. She wouldn't talk to me. She picked up her plate and headed into the living room.

I followed her. And I said:

"I am only thinking of you. That's why I asked you why were you eating this food, which is high in cholesterol and which will one day be the cause of you having a stroke."

"Dad," she said. "I'm twenty-two years old. You're in that time period now where you have to worry about that. I can kick this stuff off."

I felt like an old person then. And so I turned to leave. My daughter called out:

"Dad. Would you like a piece of fried chicken?"

"No." I sighed. "I can't afford it."

"Yes you can," she insisted.

"How?"

"Well," she said, "Renee's father takes pills."

"For what?"

And she said:

"Well, when he wants to eat what he wants to eat, he takes these pills."

I asked again: "For what?"

And she said:

"I don't know. But when he's eating boiled cauliflower and boiled stuff, he doesn't take any pills. But when he's going to have doughnuts or drink a soda or something, then he takes these pills."

And at that moment, I headed to the refrigerator to retrieve my sandwich. I was deep in thought. Pills! Of course! Why didn't I think of that before?

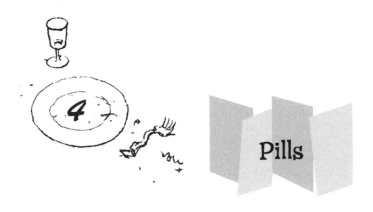

Pills

So, sandwich in hand, I went back upstairs to talk to my daughter, who was now eating Italian strawberry cheesecake and drinking a diet soda. And I said:

"Renee's father. Who is his doctor?"

And she named the doctor. And I called Renee's father's doctor and I told the doctor my problem. But Renee's father's doctor told me to call my doctor because he didn't want to interfere. So I called my doctor and I said:

"Look. Renee's father eats what he wants to eat because his doctor gave him some pills. And when he wants to eat, he takes those pills. So, for instance, when he wants to eat four slices of pizza, he will take these pills and they will wipe out all of the problems that those four slices of pizza caused."

And my doctor said:

"This is not true."

"Aha!" I shouted, thinking I had him cornered. "But if it's not true, then why is he taking them?"

"Because he *thinks* this is the way to balance out what he wants to eat," the doctor said. "But he may be taking too many pills, and whatever exam he takes the next time he may find out that the doctor doesn't want to give him any more of those pills. And it's not because his cholesterol is high but because his liver is not in such good shape."

I thought about what the doctor said and then offered a reasonable response.

"What about these pills in *moderation?*"

The doctor didn't answer right away, and I thought by using the word *moderation*—doctors love that word—that I had come up with the perfect conundrum for him. But the doctor just shrugged and asked:

"Well, then what about the pizza in moderation?"

"You don't seem to understand," I countered, by now losing my patience. "All I have had to eat is a piece of boiled broccoli and a piece of boiled cod."

The doctor said: "You're on your way."

And I said: "To what?"

And he said: "To lowering your cholesterol."

And I said: "When I lower it, what will happen?"

And he said: "You're probably going to live longer."

And I said: "But the question, Doctor, is: Will I want to?"

The doctor wouldn't give me the pills. He told me to first try lowering my cholesterol with diet and then, if that didn't work, I should come back. I don't know why doctors don't like to prescribe pills, but they don't. On the other hand, the patients feel they don't have an illness, they just have numbers. They have high numbers. And each patient says, Well, if I keep these numbers down, then I won't have anything. So I will eat the dough-nut—the doughnut with the grease and the fat and all of the sugar and the purified flour or whatever you call that flour—so they eat that. There's no nourishment in it whatsoever. The thing goes in and it makes sugar. Also, it adds plaque to the walls.

But there's a pill—in that patient's mind—there's a pill that will cover up the doughnut and lower the number. The cholesterol level is still there, but the pill knocks you down. How far down and for how long? As long as the pill lasts. Patients will not even take the pill unless they are about to eat something like that. Why? Because the pill makes them feel a little drowsy. In their mind, they're not really taking the pill.

People love pills. They medicate themselves. You've heard of people who go to the dentist and they take some kind of pill and medicate themselves before they get to the dentist. But in the case of high blood pressure there are patients who will take the pill and then eat salt and hope that the pill will keep the salt from showing up. In other words, take the high-blood-pressure pill and you can have your salt.

And there's a time to take this pill. When? People think: *When I'm going to eat some pie or when I'm going to go and eat some hot sauce or some salt. That's when I take the pill.* So the poor doctor who has prescribed these pills—who is thinking his patients are taking the pills when he says they ought to, as prescribed, along with watching the salt and flour and sugar intake—is wondering what went wrong when the patient comes back to the office with the same high numbers. That is, if the doctor is lucky enough for that person to show up. Generally the person will not show up (remember that if you don't go to the doctor, you don't have it) unless he or she has a mate who says: You've got to go.

So the person gets there and the blood is drawn and they sit around and wait and the doctor looks and even with the pills the blood pressure is still up there. So then the conversation is:

"What have you been doing?"

Now come lies all over the place.

"I've been doing exactly what you told me."

"Have you been taking the pills three times a day?"

"Yes I have."

"Well, somehow it hasn't lowered the cholesterol."

"Well, I don't know what's wrong with these pills."

"Maybe I better give you a stronger pill."

So the doctor gives the patient a stronger pill

and he takes it and then the doctor gets a call from the patient's daughter:

"My father passed out."

And then somebody in the family will eventually tell the doctor the truth.

"Look, Doctor. My father only takes this pill when he's eating doughnuts and a soda and hot sauce and some salt. And my father likes ice cream. He eats a pint of ice cream every night before he goes to bed. But he takes two double-strength pills because you told him that this pill knocks out 30 percent of the cholesterol. So he figures if he takes two that 60 percent of the ice cream is gone and then just the thought process that he might get up and work out tomorrow morning will clean out the other 40 percent. The rest of the time he's not taking the pills because he feels that they make him drowsy."

So the doctor is defeated. And so am I. Because I don't have any pills and my wife watches me closely now and she has everyone in the house watching me, so it's very hard to sneak food. Which means that all I'm left with is to find some kind of excuse. No matter how pitiful an argument it might be, I knew that I needed to come up with some reason to eat what I wanted. I needed an excuse. Like the time I was in Las Vegas with my good friend Dr. Alvin Poussaint. Alvin is a very smart man. He's a professor of psychiatry at Harvard Medical School and the Judge Baker Children's Center in Boston. So when he was up against the wall because his wife was watching him, I watched him too. Because I was sure he would come up with the most fantastic excuse. I knew he wouldn't let me down.

But he did.

Sorry
Excuses

I'm in Las Vegas, playing a hotel called the Mirage, and I'm working with the brilliant singer/entertainer Clint Holmes. We—me and Mrs. Cosby (the lovely Dr. Mrs. Cosby)—had invited two doctors as our guests: Dr. Alvin Poussaint and Dr. Tina Poussaint.

Clint and I perform and after the show the Poussaints and the Holmeses and—I can't recall Clint's wife's name right now. She was born and raised in Texas. She's got a lovely face and body, not-yet-five-six kind of height, built like the gymnast you see on TV. I can't remember her name. But she has a cute little raspy voice. And, you know, she runs the Clint Holmes empire. Not what he does onstage but the household and the children. I can't remember their names, but Clint says his kids are doing well. The way he says it is the same way as when you ask somebody's kid how they're doing, and they say: "Good." Not God's good. (Don't forget God said "Let there be light," and there was light and all God said about that was: "Good.") But good.

Anyway, we all go back up to my suite at the Mirage in Las Vegas. And there's also Ed and Carolyn Lewis—they're very wealthy. Which is good because this is a suite for very wealthy people. Its intent is to draw people who are going to throw down house-down-payment types of bets.

We decide that we want something to eat, so we push the button that calls the butler. In comes a very young blonde—I think her name was Barbara and we used to talk about Philadelphia. Barbara has a key to get into the room at any time. So in comes Barbara the butler to take our food order. Carolyn and Mrs. Cosby want watermelon. I don't know what caused it, whether the moon was shaped like a slice of watermelon that night or whatever, but they asked for "tons" of watermelon. And so they ordered two tons. Then Ed orders something that nobody would eat except a person who doesn't care if they sound boring. Something like a fruit cup. Even four slices of watermelon are more daring than a fruit cup. I mean, you might as well just go to bed if all you're going to have is a fruit cup. It's boring. And the thing is, Ed's not boring. He's the kind of guy who looks like he should have a fruit cup with hot sauce if he's going to order a fruit cup. Anyway, Ed orders a fruit cup.

Now Clint and Mrs. Holmes—*God! What is Mrs. Holmes's first name? I know she's going to be upset with me for forgetting her first name. She's genuine— she cries when something is beautiful and could give Dorothy Dandridge a tie at the finish line. What is her name?*—ordered I don't remember what. Something good and wholesome. It wasn't a burger. I think they said something like "We'll split a Reuben and strawberry ice cream and have a bottle of Château Lafite 1949."

Then Tina ordered something, I don't remember what, and then Dr. Alvin Poussaint, noted psychiatrist, said: "I'll have a pepperoni and sausage pizza."

Tina looked at Alvin and said: "Alvin??!!" (Two music notes and a bar.) She spoke his name in a tone that only a wife can say a name.

Everyone at the table turned and looked at the two Poussaints. After a moment of silence, Alvin (did I tell you he was a renowned psychiatrist?) responds to his wife's call by saying:

"What?"

Alvin had the tone of someone who is guilty but still harbors the hope that the other person is not thinking what he's thinking.

And then Tina says: "You can't have that."

To which Alvin, this respected psychiatrist, says: "Can't have what?"

At this point, I feel that I am watching a hero of mine disintegrate before everybody in the room. After all, I certainly expected more of a challenge from a man who has researched human behavior. This is when I learned that the wife-husband relationship apparently has not been studied or researched enough to protect the husband.

After a moment, Tina broke the uneasy silence.

"Alvin," Tina said. "It's going to raise your . . ."

Tina paused, looked at Alvin in a way that conveyed enormous disappointment, then added with a sigh: "Never mind."

In other words, go ahead and eat it even though it's going to give you *high* cholesterol and *high* pertension. Go ahead, eat it just before climbing into bed and give your pancreas and liver a cup of grease and saturated fat to be stored as crystals. Go ahead, eat it and the best you might hope for would be that all that fat will turn to stones as opposed to plaquing up.

Alvin looked at Barbara the butler and said in a very clear voice: "I'm going to have a pizza with pepperoni and sausage."

Tina is obviously embarrassed and there is silence in the suite.

The moment is now frozen. This is a still life.

Nobody enjoys watching a wife pull away from her husband—unless they're playing in a doubles tennis match. But Tina kind of pulled away. Finally, she spoke again: "Alvin. I said, you can't have that."

Now, there are some husbands who—knowing there are people watching—would dip very low in the male protective barrel and AT LEAST rattle the saber. But Alvin—this noted psychiatrist who is called on and visited by people from around the world who ask him for advice on human behavior—turned to his wife, Tina, and said with a little whine:

"But we're in Las Vegas, dear."

I cannot tell you how depressing an answer that was. I expected more from him. I've seen him stand up to leaders left and right. But here, up against a wife's reminder, his only defense was:

"But we're in Las Vegas, dear."

Pitiful.

Now! What was Mrs. Holmes's first name? I just can't seem to remember. What was it?

Anyway, besides excuses, another fantastic way people can fool themselves and, of course, the people around them is to have a stash. The stash is important to people who are hooked on something but know they shouldn't have it. It doesn't matter what it is—food, alcohol, cigarettes—whatever. People who have to have these things and who have loved ones around them who are watching them closely become very, very sneaky people. They lie awake at night coming up with places to hide their stash. And sometimes they can be incredibly ingenious in their deceit.

When my mother was told she had to change her diet, we all watched her. Family surveillance all over the place. But she got around it because she lived in her own house. Alone. And so she had a stash. Lamb chops. You see, lamb chops were her weakness.

Lamb Chops Were Her Weakness

My mother loved fried lamb chops. She loved fried pork chops. We used to find the bones hidden around the house because *she* knew that *we* knew that she shouldn't have them. And my mother also liked *her* fried potatoes and peppers and onions. And just to make sure they were seasoned to her liking, she would fry these things in bacon grease or lamb chop grease or pork chop grease. The point is, no matter what animal it came from, it was still grease. And grease was what my mother loved. Her whole life. And this was why the doctor was giving her pills—she had to take these pills to try to lower her cholesterol. And the doctor would say:

"Please, Mrs. Cosby. Don't eat these foods. They are very bad for you."

But my mother never listened. And the more the doctor or I would tell her that she had to change her diet, the more devious she became. Like the time her house was being constructed.

I have a place in Massachusetts, and on my property, across the driveway from where I live, there is now a fully renovated house we call "the studio." But when I first bought the property, the studio needed work. Since I decided that this would be my mother's house, I asked her what type of things she wanted in her home. What kind of heat, bathroom fixtures, etc. So one day my mother and I were standing in the unfinished kitchen—they had just installed this beautiful stove—and she looked at the stove and then she turned to me and she said:

"Bill. What I would really like is a powerful, industrial air vent over the stove so the house won't have any food odors when I steam my broccoli."

And we thought: How wonderful that was of her. But we never even thought it was for the chops, and the reason she wanted this strong air vent was to suck out the grease smoke so that no one would know what she was doing over there.

Did I say she was devious? Well, she really wasn't devious by nature. In everything else she was just so fantastic. But lamb chops were her weakness. And when someone has a weakness they will do anything. Like paying a carpenter to build a floor console–type radio with a cloth speaker guard and everything.

Except it wasn't a radio, it was a refrigerator *disguised* as a radio. I mean, anyone could look at it and think: That's a nice old floor console radio. And whenever someone would ask her to turn it on and play a little music, she would tell them it was broken. After a while, when people wondered why the radio stayed broken, my mother would say she had ordered a special part from Europe and shipments from Europe take months. And everyone just accepted what she said because no one ever thought she would lie about a broken radio. What reason could she possibly have?

Well, we eventually found out, of course, that the reason music never came out of the speaker was that refrigerators don't make sounds except for that little hum, which I guess, looking back, no one ever noticed because who would even think that someone would have a refrigerator shaped like a console radio. But my mother did. And that's where she kept her stash of lamb chops or pork chops or whatever she would find in the grocery store that she could fry.

Now, as I said, this house is situated across the driveway so I could look out my window and see it. But more to the point, *she* could look out her window and see *my* house. And she would watch. And wait. And wait. And wait. And then, when she saw all the lights in my house go out and she figured everybody had gone to sleep, she would pull out her stash of chops. She would smile at them and choose a nice big, thick one. And then she would fry it. And fry her potatoes and peppers and onions in bacon grease. And she would eat and then she would clean up meticulously.

And so the staff would go over in the morning and sometimes they would find her on the floor. They found her three times on the floor. Passed out. Cold. A mild stroke. She had mild ones. But that was it. And if someone said to her:

"Mrs. Cosby, you're having these mild strokes and I think you need to stop eating those foods."

My mother would answer:

"But I *have* to have my . . ."

Now, for all you people who've been told by your doctor that you shouldn't have this and you shouldn't have that and you should stop, and you've decided that you will, but every now and then you will have some of that and you will have some of this and then you look around and say: *Well, what do they know, it didn't seem to have . . .* And you still say: *I've got to have my . . .* Here's what I want you to do. Write the company that makes whatever it is you're not supposed to have, and say to the company:

My doctor told me not to eat this and not to drink that—whatever it is individually. Just tell the company that in spite of your doctor's warnings, in spite of all you know about the product, that you may wind up with cancer or emphysema or some disease or kidney failure, you're continuing to use their product. And just let that company know how loyal you are. Now the question is: What kind of letter are they going to send back to you? And the other thing is, if you can remember when you're on your whatever bed—maybe you've had a stroke or a setback or something horrendous or just came out of surgery— did you get a card from the cigarette company? Did the people who made the food that caused cancer send you a get-well card and congratulate you and let you know how they really appreciate the fact that in spite of what your doctor said, you continued to eat their product?

No. And neither did my mother. There's no place I could find where the pork or lamb industry ever sent her a nice letter saying:

> Thank you for going against your doctor's wishes at this time in your life. We understand that your doctor has asked you not to indulge in so many of our delicious chops, so we appreciate your continuing to eat them. However, we would like to point out that the chops are not causing the problem; rather it is what you are doing to them before you eat them. But, since we know how much you like taste over health and we see that you are still a wonderful customer and consuming and consuming and consuming, we wish you the best. As a matter of fact, we just want to thank you.

She didn't even get a note from the bacon people saying:

Dear Mrs. Cosby,

This is The Bacon Grease Company. We want to thank you—even in the face of four mild strokes—for your continued use of bacon grease in your potato and pepper and fried onion recipe. And in spite of your doctor saying that he preferred that you not eat bacon grease at this particular point in your life, your wonderful quote to him was "I've *got* to have my bacon grease." May God bless you for a long time and may your strokes always be mild ones.

Love,
The Bacon Grease Company

Anyway, I live in a house with my wife, who cannot be fooled by a stash. She would smell it, find it somehow. So what could I do in my pitiful position?

All I know is that when the mouth wants something it won't stop telling you it wants something. And in the end your mouth will turn you into a bad person. Someone who will lie to your loved ones and come up with schemes to deceive them like my mother did. But I couldn't have a stash like my mother because my wife would find it and there would be yelling. So my mouth told me:

You have to get out of the house.

And my mouth was right. So I walked over to my wife—and I was walking like a zombie, because my mouth was controlling my brain—and I said to my wife:

"My dear, why don't we dine out this evening?"

She looked at me suspiciously, but I did not fold under the pressure. I said:

"I know how you love Bouley. It's one of your favorite restaurants."

She weakened and said: "All right. Let's go to Bouley."

And then my mouth curled into a little sneer. I was about to be "Bad at Bouley."

7

Bad at Bouley

So I took my wife to Bouley—Bouley, down in lower Manhattan. She knew, of course, that my cholesterol was high. This is generally a very bad time in a husband's life when the wife hears that there is something wrong with the husband. This gives the wife the strength to tell him what to do. I don't know if this causes more love in the marriage, but I know that the wife is in control. And constantly she's saying:

"What are you eating? What is that?"

And I feel like a little boy in school with the teacher scolding me.

Now, Bouley also has a bakery, which was my

plan all along. Get near a bakery. Striking distance from a nice baked something with sugar in it.

So we went in the door leading to the restaurant, but you could also see the bakery. And I noticed in the glass enclosure that the Bouley bakery made chocolate chip cookies. And the size of them was absolutely fantastic. I had been looking for that size chocolate chip for a long, long time. You see, Famous Amos—although they are the best chocolate chip cookies you will ever eat—they're very, very small, so you have to put about three or four of them in your mouth in order to get a good taste and feel. And I don't care for the larger cookies although they are tasty and chocolatey. You have to bite and while chewing you have to hold the cookie so the chocolate begins to melt from the heat of your fingers, making a mess and leaving *evidence*. But *these* cookies seemed to be the correct size and would fit into the mouth very comfortably and have that amount already working as you chew—the correct amount of chocolate mixed with the flour and the sugar. And I saw them and Mrs. Cosby didn't.

The maître d' sat us and the waiter came over and announced that the chef had, in fact, done some marvelous things with a piece of fish. I told

Mrs. Cosby that I was going to the bathroom while the waiter explained to my wife what marvelous things had been done to this fish. Something about high altitude and leaving the fish up there for many, many years, and then bringing it back and rolling it in some kind of nuts or something using a family rolling stone. It was amazing. Just wonderful. It sounded delicious.

Obviously, I wasn't going to the bathroom. I went into the bakery. And I walked into the bakery very quickly and I stepped up and the young woman behind the counter smiled and I asked for two chocolate chip cookies. She wanted to put some rubber gloves on but I said:

"Look, dear, I don't have time. The Federales may be coming through any second. Just give them to me. I trust your hands."

And she picked them up and I just pounced on them and stuffed them into my mouth and I chewed quickly. They were delicious. My eyes rolled around and my mouth said, "Thank you so much."

I looked at the girl behind the counter and I said: "How much do I owe you?"

And she looked at me and she said something

about that was the fastest she'd ever seen anyone eat them and there was no way to tally whether I had tasted them or eaten them at all so there was no charge. And I thanked her and I went back and I sat down.

When I sat down, the waiter had gone, and now it was just a matter of getting away with what I had done. I tried to be smooth, but my wife had a look on her face that made me waver a little. See, when you're married long enough and when you have been a naughty boy, which I had been, you know that look on your wife's face. And immediately I said to myself, very quietly without moving my lips:

Uh-oh.

And I was correct. My wife said:

"Bill."

If you are married long enough, you can tell by the tone of your wife's voice when she says your name how deeply in trouble you are from one to ten. Now, my wife is like a lawyer. She doesn't say anything without knowing the answer. And so I'm always suspicious. I didn't know how much trouble I was in, but I knew that I had to play it out. I said:

"Yes, dear."

What I was really doing was preparing to carry on this conversation and ask her: "Well, what did you order for me?" But before I could say anything else she said:

"Where did you go?"

I found this to be an opening, which I used to try to deter her from going where I was afraid she was going. So I tried to play on her age and her memory. I said:

"Well, dear, I'm very very surprised and it's sort of sad that you can't remember that I told you I was going to the bathroom."

My wife came back at me—it wasn't cold, it's just that she came back—and she said:

"I *know* where you told me you were going. I *asked* you: Where did you go?"

I could only lie.

"Dear," I said. "I went . . ."

I enunciated and crossed the *t*s.

". . . to the bathroom."

She looked at me and I said calmly:

"I told you that. And that's where I went."

My wife did not blink. She didn't become cold. She just said:

"Bill. The bathroom is that way."

And she pointed in the opposite direction from where I had just been.

A sort of sweaty feeling came over me. And I bought time—valuable split seconds for my quick mind—which now was in deep, deep trouble—and I said:

"Well. Thisssss . . ."

I made the *s* sound for at least one second. And then I continued:

". . . is important for you to know, my dear, as you sit here."

And I think it's amazing how the brain can be sent scrambling for an answer while you're sitting there babbling away about something that makes no sense. It does seem to make sense, but if somebody said play that back, the tape would say: We didn't take it down.

"You're absolutely correct," I agreed. "The bathroom *is* that way, but that bathroom is for the regular people. The *celebrity* bathroom is *that* way."

And I pointed in the direction of the bakery, having scored, I thought, big-time. But once again, I should have known that a wife is like a detective. She doesn't ask a question unless she knows the answer. So then she gave me the answer. And I knew I was in deep trouble because she said my whole name. She said:

"William Henry Cosby Jr. You went into the bakery."

At that point I knew I was done and I was ready to confess. But before I could confess, she added:

"And you bought and ate a chocolate chip cookie."

And all of a sudden, the defense lawyers in my brain went scrambling saying: *She's wrong! We've got her! We got her! She's wrong! We've got an out! You did not buy that chocolate chip cookie!* So I looked at my wife, and with the swagger of a man who could draw his saber leaving the scabbard rattling away, I drew it out and I said:

"That's where you're *wrong,* my love. I did not *buy* and eat a chocolate chip cookie. And I tell you at this table, my love, may God strike me . . ."

At that time, when I said *strike,* there was a horrible sound of tables moving away from me.

People were dragging their tables away from me. Twenty to thirty people.

"May God strike me dead," I repeated, "if I *bought* and ate a chocolate chip cookie!"

My wife is a very scientific woman. You cannot defeat her. She looked me in both eyes and said:

"Let me smell your breath."

I was caught. And all I could do was promise I would do better in the future. But the thing about promises is . . .

Promises, Promises

I will do better. *I will make up for this later. This is the last time I'm going to do this.*

Fodder for promises can be found everywhere. Television can help you. There are about four hundred channels on television, and a large number of them are dedicated to health. (And then there are about forty cooking shows you can watch. These are shows you can look at while people are cooking with butter and lard and salt.) Anyway, with all this information coming at you there is one thing you *do* know from watching television. The word has gotten to you—and all of America—that oatmeal lowers one's cholesterol. You've seen the old people on TV and in commercials or infomercials or whatever telling you that oatmeal will reduce your cholesterol. (They didn't say anything about Cream of Wheat. I haven't examined that. But I do know that the man on the box of Cream of Wheat doesn't look overweight. And he's smiling. So maybe his cholesterol is low. It looks like his cholesterol is low, but looks don't mean anything.)

So, if you went to sleep after you've eaten chocolate or fat, and you've promised yourself that you're going to eat much better and you're going to be good, that the next morning you will wake up and have oatmeal, it erases all the bad.

Promises work for anything. Take exercise, for example. The doctor said I should exercise. And I said to him:

I will. I promise.

You see, beyond the lies, the amnesia, the stash, the excuses on the food front, there is the promise to yourself when it comes to exercise. And promise is the procrastinator's ally.

Now, there are rewards for exercise, and then there are different kinds of rewards for no exercise.

For example, there's a reward for sitting in one's chair in the house and maybe dozing or watching TV or reading or listening to something and then getting up and going to a couch. Even if you're just sitting there, knowing that you're not well just sitting there. And you can feel that you're not doing well. And you feel kind of like one of those goldfish you had when you were a kid and it wasn't doing well. It was somewhere between swimming and just trying to keep upright, trying to keep from floating to the top. Even then, there's a reward for all of this because you do feel good just sitting there and you've got all kinds of entertainment in front of you, entertainment at your fingertips.

You've got magazines, obviously with pictures. If there are no pictures there's a great deal of scandal, which is just as good as pictures. In regard to TV, you've got all the aerials that will pick up satellites from anyplace and give you a channel that will entertain you with anything you have, including how to sign up with the devil. And you've got six hundred channels and this remote that gives you access to these channels. Television is for entertainment and information. And then, of course, you've got DVDs and cassettes. Just in case you want to see something that the six hundred channels are not playing at the time. (By the way, many times after going through the six hundred channels, I've sat with the remote in my hand and felt like singing the George and Ira Gershwin song "I Got Plenty o' Nuttin'.")

I have a CD player that also has a remote. So if I want to put on my jazz—I already have my jazz CD set the way I want it—I just click the remote. So I am a very entertained person once I sit in the lounge chair. And the person who does this, of course, has in different places all around him things that will entertain my mouth. Beers. Sodas. Juices. Anything bagged or boxed with salt and flavorings. (Of course, I'm not supposed to eat any of those things people who sit in recliners eat, so I just sit there now with a crying mouth.) Artificial flavorings. Why people use artificial flavorings I have no idea. Did we run out of cheese somewhere? Did we run out of oranges? I don't remember anything that was so bad in Florida that we ran out of oranges. What they need to run out of are brussels sprouts.

We no longer have any brussels sprouts or brussels sprout flavoring, so in its place we are using chocolate.

So you sit there and reward yourself. You can move from what I call venues—from one venue to the other. One venue where you are sitting up—but you're reclining in a comfortable position—to another venue, onto a sofa where you can become horizontal. This is for napping. The recliner is for dozing. As a friend of mine once said, a nap is a hip nod. A doze is a not-so-hip nod. A doze is really a very vulgar thing. Nobody should really make themselves look like that. Your head literally does fall, and then you hurt yourself by catching it and snapping it back up. And then when you open your eyes you find there are about twelve people looking at you. Or, even if you're alone and those twelve people are not there, you get embarrassed and you have a conversation with yourself.

Did I fall asleep? Did anybody see me? How come I didn't notice? Why did the neck muscles let go when I specifically told them to hold the head up?

So we have that kind of reward. That feel-good promise where you promise yourself you're going to do it. You *know* you need to exercise and you *are* going to do it. But not right now because you're going to do that later. But by the time it reaches eight o'clock at night, it's not so good because you read somewhere (you think you did) that it's not good to exercise before you go to bed, and you are going to go to bed. And that's not such a good idea because your heart rate will be way up and then you get in the bed and your heart rate has to go down and you might die.

And that's just one negative about exercise. There's also another negative. How long really does it take before you can build up the good cholesterol against the bad cholesterol? This may take longer than anybody wants to live. And certainly during a workout—and that means just walking—one can hurt oneself. Many, many magazines have said that running is not good for the knees. Of course, I read these things while I was sitting down in a reclining position. Also, I became a little sleepy reading that. And I went to sleep, so I know I did retain it. You cannot run on the roads because it's bad for your knees.

Walking is good. However, how far is the question. And when you walk, how much good are you really doing? It seems questionable to walk and not really know what you're burning. And it takes so long to burn all that stuff off. So maybe it's best to just sort of cut back, which is easier to do than getting up and walking.

I feel good about the fact that I do know what I don't want to do. That's the positive of doing nothing. You don't want to hurt yourself. You don't want to go out and do too much because if you go out and you do too much and you're in a lot of pain, when you come back you're going to remember the pain that you had, the pain that you got, the pain that you self-inflicted going out trying to build good cholesterol, which you have never seen before. It's important to note that it may take longer than you really want to take. You really want more than you're actually going to get. So it is best to sit there for a little while, and this feeling of getting up and going out and doing something *will* pass. And guilt is not going to win if you are in a horizontal or reclining position, because it *is* so comfortable. You'll feel guilty for a little while, but the more you talk to yourself the more you will be able to beat the guilty feeling.

Now for the person who really exercises—this is the first time this person is really going to exercise—this is a different person altogether, because this is a person who really and truly has had enough of sitting around doing nothing. So what happens is you go up to the closet and you decide you're going to go out. Now, it depends upon the human being (and I'm not going to spend a lot of time on this), but sometimes you never get out of the house because you really don't want to go. Somehow you've had an argument with yourself, and whatever part of yourself that made you feel guilty said: *Okay, I'm going to go up and do it.* And that part of yourself has given you speeches that are similar to what your mate has said. Your mate has given you these same speeches, but now you're giving them to yourself. And you even question whether or not your mate has come into the part of yourself that is talking to you and asked you to speak to you. So you ask yourself: Who told you to tell me to get up and exercise? And so that part of you says: Well, your mate told me to do this.

So you go upstairs and you go to your closet and they're all there. Many things are there. As a matter of fact, you're quite surprised at what is there. There are birthday presents and Christmas presents from years gone by. Which really makes you realize how long your family has had an interest in having you get up and do five steps outside of the house related to some kind of exercise. You see in one of your sneakers a membership to a club that you have never ever gone to, which is not far in driving distance, but the membership is six years old and you never went. And the sneakers are six years old too. And so are the shorts. This is embarrassing because when you look at the shorts—as you hold them up—you know from just looking at them that you could never get in them.

So all of these sneakers, these shorts, these things are just not fitting well. And you find some things and your ego tells you to put them on. But when you put on things that are too small, it really shows where you're bulging in the wrong places. And you have to take those things off. And believe me, it's tougher taking those things off when you're wet than it is when you're dry.

You finally find some clothes, and these clothes you put on. And all of a sudden, with these clothes on, with the realization that you are actually going to go out, your joints begin to talk to you. There's a signal going up, coming to your brain from the different joints. They want to know what you have in mind and who's going to bear the weight? And how far they're supposed to go. So even now, in your mind—which drew up this wonderful exercise program for you that it felt was not something that could hurt you but was based on somewhere between what you used to do many, many years ago and what it thinks you can do now and what you want to do (the mind has factored all this in)—is the reality that you don't really want to do anything.

So now every joint that you have—weight-bearing joint—along with the muscles, wants to call a meeting. Oddly enough, for some reason two joints—the hips—really don't question. They don't say: *How long are we going to be out there?* But it is, in fact, the knees and the ankles who want to know: *Where are you going? How long do you plan to be out there? What is the call?*

So you promise that this particular day: *We're just going to go out for a walk. We don't care how far we go, we're just walking.* And so they all agree.

You remember that the book says stretch. So you try to do this. You bend over, and when you straighten up you find yourself a little dizzy. So that's out. But you feel if you start out slowly enough there's a natural way of stretching, and you're not going to hurt anything anyway. And so out of the house you go. The first five steps take you away from the house, and you damn near begin to feel like a child whose parents have just left. You don't know how far you're going to go out and maybe you won't get back. It's a little frightening.

So you're walking and you see people and you're headed for someplace you feel is a nice place to walk. And if you have any sense at all you start out slowly. But then you see people around you, and for some reason it seems to you these people are watching you walk. And you don't want them to look at you and feel that you're some old person. So you pick a nice gingerly pace that is your own gingerly pace. Not hurting, but your own little walking pace. You're listening to yourself and the joints. They're going but they'd like to know how far. So you make up a distance for them. And right away they say: *We don't think we can do that. Cut it in half.*

You find yourself out on a walking path—this is what you've chosen—and as you're walking you find that you've really chosen the wrong place to walk. Because these people—all of them—range in age from forty to a hundred and twelve. And whether they're coming at you or going past you, these people are faster than you. And you feel that maybe there's no place for you except on the grass. You've got to get off the trail. Because these people are speeding. And the only safe place for you is maybe in the middle. But you hear footsteps and these are quick steps and you look and passing you is some man who is old and you know he's old because of the way he's bent over. And look at his elbows and look at his arms. He's pumping away, but he is faster than you and he's not even breathing heavily. His neck seems to be coming perpendicularly out of the shoulders—straight out from between the shoulders. That's how old he is. Yet he is walking at a pace that you feel you don't even want to try to keep up with.

Now come—you can hear them behind you—two women. And they're coming and they're going to pass you and you know it. And they're talking. And they're talking about womanly things and they're not even out of breath. And they pass you. And coming at you is a lady who doesn't appear to be in good shape—she's heavy—and she's pumping and walking and huffing just a little. And here's where you begin to cry to yourself because you know that you're out of shape and you know it's going to be painful. And you feel very embarrassed, because even though these people don't say anything you can just imagine what they're thinking. To put it frankly, you want to get a T-shirt that says on the front and back: I just got out of the hospital.

So you set a pace for yourself. And your mind says: *Slow down or we're going home. Slow down. You've bitten off more than you can chew.* However, if you can just keep it in your mind that the choice of weapons is the second wind. The first negative that you're hit with is where your body actually goes into a change. You need more oxygen and your body says: *Well, wait a minute. Where are we going? What are we doing? We're walking very, very fast, and I don't think we can do this.* And all of the things start to move faster and run around and they're all complaining.

But you have to continue with this. You have to have patience. Patience working through the imaginary pain, the psychological pain. By the time you get to what is known as the second wind—as you approach that area—with the patience and keeping that pace—it's not a neck-breaking pace, it's just something that caused a change, and the lazy part of you saw this as a chance to panic. In other words, it's like somebody who went to everybody in the village and started talking badly about a person who was trying to do good and got all the village people worked up, and they lit those flames with the sticks and they came marching to stop the good person.

If you just have patience you'll notice that the pain is not the pain that the voice said it was. And one thing I think is always helpful. Just say to yourself as you begin walking: Can I keep this up all day? Obviously, you must never say no or else you'll go back home. But if you feel you can keep it up all day, then that's a wonderful, wonderful pace for you. And if you want to go faster, then obviously you're not going to be there all day. So, as you hit that second wind—I hate to give this to you—but you're now a well-oiled machine.

You'll get through that, and this is one of the
fun times of exercise. And you come back to your
house and you've broken a sweat and your shirt is
wet. You've got these trophies now. You've got a wet
sweatshirt. You've got wet shorts. The children run
away from you. But these are trophies. These are
rewards. These are the ones you want. Especially
when you go to the ice machine and you get the
plastic bags—you get about four plastic bags—
placing them on the knees and the groin and the
thighs—whatever.

And you sit down and you cover yourself up.
Now you're in the same reclining chair that the fat
person who does nothing was in. But now you're sitting there and you're fighting inflammation. And
your lungs are kind of rattling but not in a death rattle. Just in a sort of water-logged rattling. This is the
feeling of a person who has worked out. Where your
eyes are—you just have to work at focusing—not to
keep it from getting dark—but because you've been
working out. Your skin feels good. You're still sweating. You have a smile on your face. You're happy to
be back home, and as soon as you get settled into
your chair some demons jump up and begin to tell

you how many calories they *think* you burned and how you could have something sweet. Chocolatey. And salty. And pretzelly and potato chippy. Because you're going to go back out there tomorrow and you're now in that regimen. And now you can really eat what you want to eat. And you deserve to eat a lot of that today because of the work that you did. And so that's a great feeling.

But oddly enough, your reward now is not a bag of chips. Not a bag of salt. Not a bag of artificial flavoring. Not God's gift to human beings, ice cream. Your reward is now a glass of water and something to eat that is healthful.

Because you don't want to ruin what you just did. But still, I have to be careful, because at age sixty-five, I'm working with old parts.

Old Parts

My father was the first person I heard refer to the human body as a machine. When the subject of eating habits came up, my father, William H. Cosby, Sr., said:

"You cannot put the same load on a sixty-five-year-old truck that you used to put on a five-year-old truck."

And then he said: "Any math teacher will tell you that the first weight carried by a new vehicle is relative to that vehicle's performance thirty years later."

Well, I was very young—I was about seven or

eight years old—and I was a new machine, so first of all, I didn't even believe what my father had said because I had trust and faith in God that God would not be General Motors or anything like that. I just didn't see that being possible. But at age sixty-five, it is quite believable and understandable.

So there I was, sixty years after my father's pronouncement that the body was a machine, sitting in my den, sweating. Sweating, by the way, for no reason. (Sweating for no reason is a wonderful sign that your thermostat is off.) But that's not really true. You don't sweat for no reason. Once you reach a certain age you sweat because the body is trying to tell you something. And I remember being very, very embarrassed when the truth was spoken to me. Spoken to me not by a medical practitioner but by a man fifteen, sixteen years older than I. And I did not ask him to go as deeply as he went into this discussion of certain ailments. As far as I was concerned this was to be a sort of humorous discussion. But he went serious. (Although he thought he was being funny.) Anyway, he hit me in a place I didn't want to go. What he said was that at age sixty-five, I, meaning my body, had old parts.

Old parts. What happens when you have old parts? Well, for one thing, you get pains you never had with new parts. What causes these pains? Do we really know? If you're not a doctor, you don't know what a pain represents. But we do know that there are certain kinds of pain and you can describe them in terms of the length of the pain. For example, the pain that's very short.

All right. You get a pain and it's a hit and you say to yourself: *Whoa! What was that?* You ask yourself. And your self says: *Well, that was a pain.* Well, where was it? *It was someplace in the back.* Well, was it the back? *No, I don't think it was. It was more in the area of the soft tissue.* (I learned that term from talking to different doctors. Soft tissue as opposed to hard tissue, which is, I think, gristle. And it might be bone. Those two I think. I'm not sure.)

So, anyway, there's this shot and then it goes away. Just a little thing that hit. Well, you don't examine that. You don't say: Well, why did that hit? What made that happen? Why did it go away? What did I do? You just know that it happened. And it hurt. And then it went away. Old parts.

Now, there's another pain that can hit and it stays a while. This usually is muscular but it can also be in an organ. Now, there are many soft tissue organs—and I don't know if I'm being redundant or redumbdent—but this pain hits and it just stays, maybe lasting fourteen seconds. (Which, when you're having pain, is a lifetime, depending on your level of tolerance.) It hits big and then it starts to subside. Old parts.

Then there's the pain that says: Well, I think you better sit down and get some help. This is accompanied by loss of light with the eyes open. But that pain too eventually goes away. Old parts.

Now, these are the kinds of pain doctors don't even try to explain to us. I'm not saying whether or not we would listen, but I'm just saying why not, when you go to have a physical (and I'm being serious but I'm not being *so* serious), why not keep a little chart as your parts get old? A chart that says: You know, I had something and it went away. What does the doctor say about something you had and it went away? I mean, why did it come there in the first place? Well, I can only assume—obviously I'm not a doctor—the only thing I can assume is that it could've been a wrinkle. Because when you've got old parts, sometimes old parts bend or they wrinkle. And they get caught and then they straighten out. So it might have been the straightening out of something that caused the pain. Or it could've been something that got pinched for no reason and then straightened out. Or while it *was* pinched the pain was there. Whatever caused it, *something* happened.

I've felt things and *heard* joints as my parts got old. A simple pain would suddenly appear. For example, your hand is up at your face and then you bring your arm down and you hear a snap. Which, if you've heard it on any football field, would mean something was broken. But because these are old parts, old bones, they're able to make that sound and really nothing is hurt. It's just the grinding of old parts.

So don't be afraid to ask your doctor about your old parts. See what the doctor has to say. I just think it might be very, very interesting. You say to a doctor: Look. I straightened my arm out the other day and it went SNAP! And there was no pain that went along with it. There was no paralysis. There was just a very large sound. Loud. As a matter of fact, people came from far away and asked: Are you all right? Some of them thought I had dropped something. I said: No. It was just my arm. I straightened it out. And they said: You felt no pain? And I said: No, I felt no pain. I was able to pick up the phone. Bend my arm back and forth.

I've also heard it in the ankle. I've had it at times when I was just sitting in a chair and I heard it. I have this wonderful blue leather chair with a footrest. And there were times when I would be watching TV and I'd just kind of move my right ankle—I would say no more than two or three inches—I'd just move the right ankle. And CRACK! But there was no pain with it. So now I'm used to this. The first couple of times that I heard it, I looked down to see if anything was out of joint. But it was just old parts.

Sometimes old parts make strange sounds. Gurgling sounds. Some of these sounds are coming from the intestines, I think. And this depends on whether I've eaten. Generally, I like to eat my protein first and then my vegetables. And I don't get those sounds as much if I eat chocolate first and then nothing else after. But if I don't eat chocolate, then I begin to sound like a musical instrument. I can do a guitar with a wa-wa pedal. And there are many songs that my old parts have played. But there's no rhythm to it. It's just gurgling things. It's an angry stomach. And an angry pancreas. Whoops! There it is. I just got one. And it traveled a distance—about four inches. But it was a soft, sort of purring sound. The kind of sound you get when your cat is next to you. You hear it breathing but it has that rattle sound.

Wait! I just heard another one around the back. I don't know what that was, but it sounded like something in there that had to do with food. Solids and liquids. It's just old parts. So all of these things will take care of themselves. (I don't think that's really true. I just don't want to worry about all these things.) But I think it's important to tell your doctor: I had a shot of pain. Just had it once. What was that? Just see what the doctor says. Surely, in medical school, they had to have covered the subject: pains that go away. I mean, there has to be a class in that.

Sometimes it hurts and you never hear from it again. And then sometimes it will hurt and it won't happen again for another year. And it's the same thing. So how bad is something that happens once a year? Did you tell the doctor about it? No, I just dismissed it and it went away. I mean, even if you told a doctor, what would they give you for something that happens once a year? The conversation would probably go something like this:

PATIENT: I have this pain.

DOCTOR: Well, how often do you get this pain?

PATIENT: Once a year.

DOCTOR: Is it the same day?

PATIENT: No, but pretty much a year goes by and then I have it.

DOCTOR: Well, is there any paralysis with it?

PATIENT: No, but it made me feel like if it had continued I would have to go down on one knee.

DOCTOR: How long did it last?

PATIENT: It didn't stay that long.

DOCTOR: Was it in the joint?

PATIENT: No! It was in the soft tissue area.

DOCTOR: Don't worry. It's just old parts.

Dismissal. It's one's dismissal. You dismiss a pain. You stand up quickly to eliminate a sharp pain. For about a second. Then you dismiss it. You say: Well, that didn't hurt. But it *did* hurt. And *why* did it hurt?

And so, from the moment my friend told me that, at age sixty-five, I had old parts, these parts had come into focus. The same old parts my father had mentioned when I was young, the old parts that in my youth seemed a thousand years away, were here. And now I had them. Old parts. They had come into focus in my mind. The old parts I had refused to acknowledge. So what should I do now? I have already told you that I have reached a point and place in my mind where I know that the doctors with their examinations can find things that you don't want to have. And I don't want to have anything. And so the solution to these pains suddenly became very clear. There was only one thing to do. Gamble. That's right. Make a bet with yourself that these pains mean nothing. And so, like someone sitting at a blackjack table staring at two very low cards, I looked up at the mirror and said:

"Hit me!"

Gambling with Yourself

Obviously there's a point when you decide that you can heal yourself. And this is not a flu shot. You can think of yourself as not wanting a flu shot but perhaps *needing* a flu shot. And the odd thing about one's mind is that if you take the flu shot, and you don't get the flu, you tend to pose the question: Now, would I have gotten the flu or not gotten the flu had I not taken the flu shot? The flu shot stings—it hurts for about thirty seconds. But the flu can last at least ten days, and the worst thing that can happen is next year you don't need it because you're dead. And so the next year you decide to take a gamble. You roll the dice and you don't get the flu shot. And you find yourself blowing into your hands and shouting things like "baby needs a new pair of shoes!" Yes, you are clearly rolling the dice even though I think it's something that you don't realize. You don't see yourself rolling the dice. You don't see yourself gambling. But you do see yourself taking a chance. And what you don't want to admit, what you don't want to focus upon in your mind, is that you have become a gambler with your own body.

And so, the gambler I have become brings me back to the simple premise that not having something or *thinking* that you don't have something is better than having it. And so logic then dictates that it's not important to check out something that's giving you a warning signal. And the odds tell you that too. Because many times doctors will say (after the examination: i.e., blood drawn, X rays, swabs they put on a petri dish and then into the incubator, etc.) that you don't have it. Maybe some sort of medication needs to be taken, some pills or whatever, but you don't have it. So the odds are on your side. And the one thing a gambler lives for is getting odds.

Okay. You may be saying: "But I'm not a gambler." Really? Let's take tennis, for instance. If you play tennis, then you know that in playing tennis the great-looking shot is the volley down the line as opposed to a safer volley that you're sure will land somewhere on the court. But that volley down the line, if you make it, can lift your spirits and cause you to feel fantastic and strut around the court thinking: "I am the greatest tennis player in the world!" However, most B tennis players can only make that shot 13 percent of the time. Yet it's that one time when you *do* make it—when you take that gamble and it pays off—that keeps you trying to make it again. The same thing with golf. If a pro hits the ball into the rough and behind a tree, he will chip back onto the fairway. But a duffer will stand over his ball, behind that tree, squint his eyes through the branches so he can catch a glimpse of the green, and then decide he's going to hit the golf ball over the second branch, under the third branch, and around the trunk. He shouldn't even be trying a shot like that, but he's thinking that if he makes it, he will feel wonderful.

There are things as you live with yourself—

medically or functionally pertaining to your body—things that you look at and keep fuzzy-looking on purpose. You don't allow them to come into focus and be clear because if you do, that's going to be frightening. This fuzzy focus allows you to eat improperly. The fuzzy focus allows you not to get up and exercise, even though when you were in your twenties, to walk would be an embarrassment in terms of what would be called exercise. At sixty-five, it *is* exercise. Why? Because we're not in college anymore. That's why. We're not on the football team anymore. We're not even intramural anymore. We're not even remedial anymore. We have old parts. And we don't really want to focus on these parts.

If you keep things out of focus, you're going to be able to eat those pieces of chocolate that are on your pillow. There are two pieces of chocolate on your pillow in your hotel room. And you look at them and you say:

"It's midnight. Should I really eat sugar? And where did they get these chocolates? Why are they giving them to me for free? Certainly the hotel has included these two pieces of chocolate on the bill. They're probably charging me five dollars for these things, so I better eat them. But if I eat these two little cubes—which are smaller than the squares on a portable chessboard—how much sugar am I eating?"

Out of focus! Don't focus in on that!

Okay, so I eat one and I say:

"That tasted pretty good."

And then I eat the other one and throw the paper away. And I tell myself:

"Okay, I ate them. They probably charged me five dollars and I ate the five dollars' worth of chocolate. Which is pretty good, because those two pieces of chocolate are nowhere near five dollars' worth of chocolate."

And then your sweet tooth—no one ever showed me which tooth is the sweet tooth but we must have one because everybody keeps talking about it; anyway, your sweet tooth is activated and you go to the minibar in the hotel room for more chocolate. You know you shouldn't do it—more chocolate might raise your blood sugar and might radically raise your blood pressure so that when you get in the bed you've given yourself high blood pressure and you know that you could have a stroke. But if you keep that fact out of focus, it won't worry you. That's helpful, if you keep it out of focus. Because if you keep it in focus, you might worry about it. So as you're keeping things out of focus, that helps you to eat improperly. To gamble with your old parts. And you can use a convenient loss of memory to help you do this. For instance: When did I last eat? (See: "Once in a While" for more details on this wonderful method.) If you keep everything out of focus, you can eat whatever you want. You don't have to wait for a certain time. You just can't remember when you last ate. Especially if you had an appetite. And it's also convenient not to be able to remember whether or not something is good for you. So you keep that out of focus too. And you're gambling that it won't hurt you.

So you see, there's excitement in taking a chance, something exhilarating about gambling. And the excitement of playing—the exhilaration of gambling—with one's health is the same thing. And why a person would want to do that is quite obvious. Because most of the time we don't realize how low the chips are getting and we really don't want to know. If you're standing at a craps table and you start with a hundred dollars—and let's say that hundred dollars is your body and your health—then as you're gambling you can see that you only have thirty-five dollars left. But with your body, you can't really see that—it doesn't show up. We don't know when it will become evident that we've only got two dollars left. Then there are some people—the way they gamble— they only have two dollars left, and then they look and see that they owe another twenty dollars of vigorish (commission) that they were charged while they were losing.

And speaking of losing, there is something I'm losing that is troubling me. I'm losing my hair. What does that mean? All I know is that it frightens me.

Why Is
There Hair?

I want to know why we don't know more about hair. What is it about hair that we have it and we know it's got something to do with the health of the body but we ignore it. Sure, people can say: *Well, it's not bothering anybody, it's not killing anyone.* How do we know? We're always so busy studying cells and cloning people and splitting genes. Why can't we figure out how and what hair means to the human body? And I'm talking about hair. I'm not talking about skin. Although there is also a problem with skin. As you get older, you don't have oil. The skin is drier. I don't know why. But I want to know. I want *you* to know. I want you to ask your doctor. For now, however, we are talking about hair.

What does a person gain or what does a body lose when hair falls out? When there's baldness that starts at a certain age (could be an early age, could be a late age), what is going on? Somebody tell me. I don't understand because I happen to believe that a great deal of the human story is in hair. Why does a person turn gray? Is there something missing? It's obvious we're losing something. Is it shortening my life? Is it lengthening my life? Why did I lose my hair color? Not only on top but in my nose, in my ears. I believe that hair can have its own thought processes. Why is it that when I was young I had no hair—on my back. And now that I'm in my sixties it's all over my back. What am I turning into?

I first lost it on top of my head. It receded. It receded and then the hair came out of my back. I lost it on my head—it started to thin out—and then it came out of my ears. It's growing out of my eardrums. Hair. And gray hair. It's in my nose. Gray hair. But I didn't lose my beard. Why did it come off the top of my head? What is that a sign of? Old parts? Not necessarily. Because there are young people who started to become bald at an early age. And I think the place you need to start to examine in order to find the answers is clearly in the experimentation of how to grow the hair. Because there are certain medications that were given to people and it was claimed that these medications would make hair grow. But they also had warnings on the labels that said things like: If you take this product you might grow hair but you will eradicate something else in your system.

So anyway, I lost hair. And I'm saying there's something wrong here. Because along with the loss of hair, it started receding. It receded and then it stopped. Thank goodness it stopped. But I've also lost hair in places where in my youth I had hair. I have no hair on my calves anymore. I used to have hair there. I have maybe two hairs left on each side. And I think these hairs are there to help me find things in the dark. When my shinbone comes close to something I can't see, the hairs touch it and let me know I'm about to bang into whatever it is. So I think these hairs are protective things.

I still have hair across the toes—the two big toes. There's hair there, on the top of them. And I have hair on top of the hands. But I've lost some hair across the backs of my hands, the overside of the palm. The hair on my forearms is not as much as it was when I was young. It has, as we say, thinned out. And it also weakens. Hair can become weaker in the support structure of its old self. For example, the eyebrows. I noticed that my eyebrows now are coming more into view for me to see while they're hanging there. They're drooping. They're coming over the eye. The hair is just limp now. The eyelash hair is limp. Except for the gray ones. They tend to go up more and away from the others.

I do remember that there were some eyedrops I took and the warning on the label said that there might be thickening of the eyelashes. And it did happen. I took the drops for a while. And one day I was frightened because I looked in the mirror at my right eye (which is where the drops were going) and I thought there was a caterpillar crawling across my face.

Clearly there are some hairs that have some sort of dementia and have forgotten how to grow. Because I am *still* able to grow hair. The hair on my back, for example, is growing fine. And because of the hair, which is filling in at the coccyx bone, I know I'm still able to grow hair. I think that upon my death, when they turn my body over and they do whatever they do, if they just take the skin and lift it off the coccyx bone, they will find that the coccyx bone is still growing hair. Hair will be coming out of the coccyx bone like a Chia Pet.

So I decided to do some research about hair loss. I know I said earlier that this book wasn't based on any research, but when I started to think about hair I realized I knew less than nothing, which is about the same as most people. The first thing I came across was put out by a group called the Academy of Family Physicians. According to them, about 10 percent of your hair is resting while the rest is growing. So does the resting hair fall asleep and then fall off your scalp? I couldn't find an answer. And then I saw that your thyroid gland can cause hair loss if it is overactive *or* underactive. So I looked up *thyroid gland* in *Webster's Third New International Dictionary* and here is a partial definition of the thyroid gland:

> . . . having a profound influence on growth and development . . . specifically stimulating the metabolic rate . . . has complex interrelations with the pituitary and adrenal and other endocrine glands.

Complex interrelations? This made me feel I clearly understood now that you can go bald because you don't have enough or too much of whatever this was that I just read.

And then there were all these other things I found in my research that can cause hair loss. Illness. Stress. Hormonal problems. Pregnancy. (At least I know that's not why I'm losing hair.) Certain medicines. Too much vitamin A. Fungal infections. Tight hairstyles like pigtails and cornrows. (Haven't worn either, so that can't be it.) And finally, "common baldness." Or, as it is also known, "male pattern baldness."

I have common baldness. I hate to think there is anything about me that's "common." But I guess my baldness is common. Common baldness. I know what *common* means, but then I started to wonder what exactly was the definition of *baldness*. So I went back to *Webster's Third New International Dictionary* and I looked up *bald*. The definition was: "Lacking all or a significant portion of the natural or usual covering of hair on the head or sometimes on other parts of the body." (But this is not true, Mr. Webster, because automobile tires don't grow hair.)

It also said that a mountain can be bald due to lack of foliage and a bird can be bald if it loses its feathers. But the first definition about loss of hair pertained to me and described me perfectly. Common baldness. I have it. And this is one thing I can't dismiss like the sharp pains that come along once in a while. I can't dismiss it because I see my common baldness every day in the mirror. So how can I fix it? The thing is, you can't fix common baldness. You can take medication, but then other things happen to you that aren't good.

What about gray hair? It must be a sign of something wrong. Is it fixable? Why does it happen?

In my research I found an article from *Popular Science* written by a woman named Anne Marie Hathcock. The article was edited by Bob Sillery and researched by Reed Albergotti, Rob Barnett, and Emily Bergeron. (With all those credits, I figured it must be a good article.)

The article referred to a doctor from the University of Bradford in England—the doctor's name was D. J. Tobin—who said gray hair was part of genetics and aging. Old parts? It looks that way. Apparently, there is a chemical called melanin that is produced by cells in the hair follicles. And this chemical gives hair its color. As we get older, the cells stop making melanin. Why? Do cells have old parts too?

Anyway, since we don't have a gland that produces melanin, when these cells get tired and stop producing melanin, the hair turns gray. Why do the cells stop making what they're supposed to make? Nobody knows, since melanocytes and melanosomes, the "building blocks" of melanin, are still there in the follicles when the hair turns gray.

So researchers have yet to come up with a reason why hair follicles stop producing melanin. I think that's wonderful! Gray follicles contain everything they need. They just stop. All of a sudden they stop making it. And I feel that is a great answer. I like this guy very much. Because at least someone is telling me that they know that it just stops. They don't try to go around the bush with a mile-long definition of what happened. This fellow's definition clearly says he doesn't know why hair stopped making it but it's no longer there.

But there was no signal, no sign of weakness I ever noticed when I was losing the melanin. And you can't find melanin in cantaloupe or honeydew or any of the melon family. Have they tried eating hair with color? I think that maybe—if we could find someone who could (and I'm not suggesting this), I'm suggesting that this person be paid and, upon the onset of gray hair, that this person eat a handful of hair every day. *Colored* hair, by the way. And he could eat his own hair. Put melanin back into his body again. So the question is: Can melanin be recycled by eating one's own hair? And a man could do that by growing a long mustache and just, every two days, biting off the end of his mustache as it dripped over his lip.

As the article went on it said that some scientists feel "free radicals, which are produced by various metabolic processes within our body (including melanin production), can cause DNA damage."

So free radicals may be attacking the hair. Where do these free radicals come from? From Reed College? From Cal Berkeley?

Perhaps gray hair is the result of a person being frightened many times during infancy and child-hood. Just being playful—a little child who loves being scared—could lead to building reckless free radicals within the melanin.

And so, after all my research, I now know I am low on melanin and full of free radicals. But what if I had never done anything bad to myself? What if I hadn't eaten so much fat? Would I still be losing my hair? Which made me wonder: What if I cloned myself and kept the clone in a completely healthy environment?

Bill Clonesby

A **Bill Cosby clone?** Why not? You can do all the things with this clone that never would have happened. No fast foods. No cigarette smoke around him. This is going to be a wonderful person. You're going to read to him every night and make sure that he studies and give him that kind of environment.

But cloning has a lot of problems.

There was a baby girl who was supposed to have been cloned and the news caught the media off guard. The media were shocked and surprised. Television shows were very hostile to the people who claimed to have cloned this child. Everyone asked the clone people to show some evidence, but (as I am writing this) they never came forward with any proof. In fact, the clone people wouldn't let doctors examine this baby—whom they called Eve—because, according to the clone people, the parents (or was it parent?) were afraid of some sort of custody issue.

These clone people went on television and, without showing any particular proof, just said they cloned someone. If this were true, then I think the medical profession should have gone to where the supposed clonee was and just greeted the people, said some friendly hellos, then pointed to the sky and said: "Look up there!" And when they all turned to look, Dr. Biopsy Cloverdale—one of the fastest doctors with a scalpel—could have used the scalpel to take a tissue sample from the hand of the child which could then have been passed quickly to Dr. Urpen—the greatest biochemist in the world—and he could have put the tissue sample in a petri dish, covered it, slipped it into the pocket of Dr. Chichazfrick Putasty with 1,200 dyes. All in a matter of 2.9 seconds. Then the tissue sample could have been quickly whisked away by some postal service and insured for $7.95, the price of the petri dish. But how much and what do you need in order to prove that a person is the exact clone of another person? Is it all in hair? Is it dandruff? Is it: Here, wipe your nose and then get the other one to wipe her nose?

Anyway, the attacks in the media were extremely vitriolic. As a result, I, the viewer, never did get any information because the clone people were brought on these talk shows and they were ridiculed and dismissed as frauds. And for the first time you actually saw what would happen if a spaceship landed on Earth. What I mean is, they were given so much attention and the story became so convoluted that it was impossible to figure out what was real and what wasn't real. And one began to wonder that if cloning was so simplistically rebukable, why even acknowledge these people except to say: *More news at eleven.*

The answer is, of course, that television made a lot of money depicting these people as fakes. The television people have always known that the best way to make someone look fake is to ask a question and then let the person talk. And then, before they can even answer the *first* question, ask *another* question that begins "but don't you think?" And when the person starts to answer the second question just cut the person off and attack them for not answering the first question. That way the media can not only make a person look bad but also frustrate the viewer. I don't mean to say that I wanted to hear what the clone people had to say because I believed in cloning. I only wish to point out that I wanted to be entertained by the answers because I was watching television and that's what television is supposed to do—entertain. After all, we had a live, talking, tabloid star for once. Why not let them entertain us, the viewer?

So I began to think—and I don't know much about cloning so I will not get into how many embryos are destroyed because of this—but I began to think about cloning. And I figured it would be a long, long time before anyone began to clone Africans or African Americans. (Unless slavery came back.) But if *I'm* cloned—or anyone is cloned—what is the purpose? Or if you clone sheep—which they did with the famous Dolly—why are you cloning sheep? You are cloning sheep for what reason? I mean, you already have ten thousand head of sheep. How many bad sheep have you? To shear? (I don't understand what I'm talking about, I'm just asking myself questions.)

So they were successful with a sheep. They cloned a sheep. But she has wound up with arthritis even though her mother didn't have arthritis. So much for cloning. If the mother didn't have arthritis and the clone had it, then the clone went bad, didn't it? So what good is cloning sheep? Isn't it better to clone things you can control, like earthworms? That's a simple organism. Or how about a fly?

Now, all this cloning business is in the news and I'm looking at myself. If you cloned me, what would be important about cloning me? It occurred to me that one of the things that might be exciting about cloning people who are well-known is that the clone might grow up and not want to be known for the thing that the well-known person was famous for doing. So we would be able to develop from that cloned person something different from the original.

How many people have you heard say:
Well, I'm more than just . . .

Or somebody in show business who says:

Well, you know, I'm not going to do that anymore.

So what are you going to do?

Well, I just want to be such and such.

In other words, what if my clone decided he didn't want to be a comedian? What if my clone decided he wanted to be a singer? People would look at my clone and say:

Yeah, but he looks funny. I'm sorry but I can't help it because he looks just like Bill Cosby, so I just start laughing. I really can't take him seriously as a singer. You know, as a Frank Sinatra. Or as a Nat King Cole.

So there is my clone, taking dance lessons and singing lessons and hip lessons because my clone doesn't want to be Bill Cosby, he wants to be Sammy Davis Jr. He's six foot one, 180 pounds, and the clone wants to be Sammy Davis Jr.

But they've already cloned a Sammy Davis Jr. And the Sammy Davis Jr. clone looks exactly like Sammy Davis Jr. And he's mad at the Bill Cosby clone, who's trying to outdo him. Or maybe the Sammy Davis Jr. clone doesn't want to be Sammy Davis Jr., he wants to be Bill Cosby. But the public is rejecting these clones because they still want the original.

Even if clones wanted to be what the original was, that would still be a problem. For example, if you had an Elvis Presley clone, that clone would probably want to be Elvis Presley. In fact, all of the Presley clones would want to be Elvis. But the public would get tired of that because everywhere you looked there would be Elvis. And *exact* Elvises. You'd have the Elvis Tabernacle Choir.

Sophia Loren. Think about Sophia Loren cloned. You could have Marilyn Monroe clones. And these clones would want to be astronauts and go up in space. You see, these clones would not want to be known for their looks. They would want to be known for their brains. And no fooling around. But it would be tough on the public to look at them and say:

I accept you for being the chess champion, Marilyn Monroe.

Or what if the Marilyn Monroe clone wanted to become president? Could we accept her singing "Happy Birthday to You" to herself?

Certainly there is the possibility.

Personally, I would want to clone the people

who frightened me when I was young. Scary people from the movies. Boris Karloff, Bela Lugosi, Peter Lorre, Vincent Price. See, you don't have any more Boris Karloffs so you need a Boris Karloff clone. A Bela Lugosi clone. And so on. But it could get scary. What if the horror movie clones turned around and decided—like the characters they played in the movies—to attack people. You would have the attack of the clones looking for spare parts that really belonged to the original cloner. After all, Dolly the sheep's mother was healthier than Dolly the sheep. In fact, Dolly the sheep developed arthritis at an early age. So if the clones were defective why wouldn't they come after the originals to replace their bad parts? And that would be the opposite of what it was supposed to be.

So unless we're cloning just for spare parts—which seems to be backward—why are we doing this? And since Dolly the sheep died very young, how do we know the clone's spare parts are good enough for the original piece to stay alive?

So looking for a perfect match of yourself may not be such a good idea. Speaking of matches, do you have a light?

Smoking

Smoking is bad for you. And that statement doesn't need any elaboration. We all know it. I mean, why else have cigarettes been called "coffin nails" since the day they came out?

In the beginning, I think we must all remember, those of us who had our first cigarette, those of us who inhaled the first time, that when you had those first couple of puffs you became dizzy and nauseated. Only a human would go back to that again. But to be sick and nauseated seems to be no warning to a human being. To be dizzy to the point where your eyes can't focus—now this is a warning by anyone's definition. I mean, if you put some food in your mouth, if you had some soup and you took two sips and you felt it go down to your stomach and you felt dizzy and you couldn't focus and you noticed you started to sweat and you became nauseated, you would say there's something in this soup, and you'd push it away. So smoking does tell you something and you tell yourself something. Smoking tells you that it's bad for you. But you tell yourself and your body:

Pay no attention to the feeling. It will go away once we get used to the smoke.

And then that's when the fun begins. Your body wants it more and more. And you don't get dizzy or nauseated anymore because the body is really liking the nicotine. You have an addicted body. And once that happens, smokers act like crazy people.

For example, the other day I was in Massachusetts, in the guest house, talking to a friend who had come to visit. In the middle of our conversation, the phone rang. So I answered the phone and it was my wife, so I had to talk to her. My wife has always hated smoking. In fact, since I stopped smoking cigars a few years ago, she won't allow smoking in any of the houses on the property. But my friend is a smoker. So the minute I got on the phone he seized the opportunity, motioning to me, as if he was only going outside to give me privacy while I talked with my wife. I knew, however, that he was just using me as an excuse because I was on the phone. I could hear him thinking:

Well, while he's on the phone I will go outside and I will have a smoke.

And so my friend slipped on a coat and walked outside. The problem was, it was twelve below zero. Twelve below zero! At night! Wind howling! Snow falling! It was the kind of weather you see on these documentaries about the Arctic Circle or the North Pole. They even had a warning on television earlier in the day that said: Bring your pets inside. They had emergency numbers on the screen during the news in case people lost the heat in their house or got stuck on the road. But my friend had to have a smoke. And so he just put on his coat and walked out into the night. And I remember thinking that the next time they decide to go on a polar expedition, they should get smokers. They could even have smokers pulling the sleds when the dogs got too cold. Because there was my friend—I could see him out the window—standing in a blizzard, sucking in minus-twelve-degree air along with the smoke. Whether or not he finished the whole cigarette, I don't know. But obviously however many puffs he took to get that nicotine feeling in his body before his fingers froze and fell off must have been worth it to him. Why else would someone risk hypothermia and frostbite?

I finished talking with my wife and my friend came back inside with a wind-chapped face. And I asked him:

Do you ever hear yourself breathe? Do you ever hear a whistling or a wheezing sound when you're breathing?

And he said:

I couldn't hear myself breathing. The wind was too loud.

And I could see that his brain was frozen, so I repeated the question and explained that I didn't mean while he was outside, I meant ever. And he said that yes, once in a while there is a little wheezing. And I asked him if he had a cigarette cough, especially in the morning. And he said, yes, he did.

Now, those of you who live with a smoker know

the sound of that cough. It sounds like the person is dying. But in between coughs, what do they do? Right! They light a cigarette.

Anyway, I asked my friend if he had physicals and he said he did, once a year. And I asked him if, when they drew blood, it made him nervous about his cholesterol, and he said it didn't. How about the urine sample in terms of diabetes, kidneys, whatever? That didn't bother my friend either. So finally I asked him:

What about the chest X ray?

A look of abject terror washed over my friend's face and he became very pale. I thought he was going to faint. And I knew that was his Achilles' heel. You see, as my friend explained it, every time he goes for a physical and he steps up to the chest X-ray machine, he begins to shake. And the doctor has to calm him down. Once, my friend said, the doctor came in after taking a chest X ray and told him they had to take another one. My friend said he swooned, thinking there was something they wanted to get a closer look at. He said to the doctor:

Please, don't show me, Doc. And even if I have it, don't show me.

But the problem was only that my friend was shaking so much during the X-ray exposure, the rippling motion of his terrified body had caused the X ray to come out blurred.

And that's the funny thing about smokers. (And I used to be one, so don't accuse me of preaching.) Smokers know smoking is bad for them. The morning cough tells them it's bad, the way they feel after a two-pack night tells them it's bad, but they have some chemical in the brain that keeps the message from getting to the part of the brain where common sense is stored. They tell themselves: Don't worry about it. It's just a cough. It will go away. Well, of course it will go away if you don't pay any attention to it.

So there's your adjustment: You didn't pay attention. But how did you justify not paying attention to it. When you heard the wheezing, that little whistle, and you said, Wait a minute, that's me, what happened? Well, what happens is that very quickly the adjustment cells of your brain came in, like insurance adjusters, and they came in and the conversation went like this:

BRAIN: What's the problem?

SMOKER: There's a little whistle that came up for no reason.

BRAIN: So what are you going to do about it?

SMOKER: I'm not going to pay attention to it.

BRAIN: Okay. Good. I was worried there for a minute.

And that's how it goes. We get rid of everything by not paying attention to it.

Colds become a problem for smokers because if you have a chest cold, you will still get the urge to smoke a cigarette, despite the fact that you have a chest cold and your lungs are fighting for their life. And so that's what menthol cigarettes were made for. These cigarettes were made for people to smoke when they had a cold because they contained menthol, which is supposed to help a cold. Here you are with the cilia in your lungs and the peri-something or other, and they're weakened and there's bacteria running all through and white blood cells fighting and beating the stuffing out of one another and you decide you still want to put some smoke in there. So the cigarette people said:

We'll put some menthol in a cigarette and make it cool like a breath of fresh air.

So even if menthol cigarettes aren't their brand, when a smoker gets a cold they run out and buy menthol cigarettes. And they light up and they inhale and that menthol-filled smoke hits their lungs and their lungs say:

What the hell is this?

And the lungs get even weaker. It feels like a giant ice cube in their lungs and puts things in a knot so that it hurts across the board. But they still smoke.

Now this behavior—the way smokers think— makes them want to congregate. And when you go into a room of smokers where everybody's allowed to smoke in that room, you immediately can smell the smoke, and you're inhaling everybody's smoke, it's thick, and your eyes are watering. You ever been in a room like that? Of course you have. And if you're a nonsmoker, the first thing you want to do is get out of that room. But the first thing a smoker does is light up a cigarette too. So, if you're a smoker, that's what you do. Light up your own cigarette, and you're just smoking and there is some part of you that says:

Man, this room is smoky. So there's a part of you that makes no sense to yourself. But then again the question is: How much smoke does it take for you to want to not light up your own cigarette?

I would contend the answer is that if you walk into a smoky room and you light up your own cigarette in that smoky room—a room that was made smoky by other people smoking their own cigarettes—then that secondhand smoke, even though it is dangerous, is not as fulfilling as your own smoke.

Now if you could slip into the mind of a smoker (and once again, I *was* a smoker so don't accuse me of being on a high horse), what would you find? You'd find a brain trying to send a message to the person, and that message is: Quit! I don't think I ever met a smoker who, when they really looked at themselves, didn't want to quit. All smokers want to quit. And not just for health reasons. Smokers stink, and they know it.

One thing's for sure, when you *do* finally stop, and I'm five years removed from cigar smoking, your nose clears up and you can smell things again. For the past two years, I've really been able to pick up smokers' odors. Not just their breath. I'm talking about picking it up on their clothes, their hair, and virtually anything with which they come in contact. If you're no longer a smoker or have never been a smoker, then to walk into a hotel room where a smoker slept is a horrible experience. Some of the hotels do their best to eliminate the smell by using industrial solvents and cleaning methods. But all they've done is to mask the smell and perfume the carpet with the aroma of four-day-old Lysol. And despite their efforts, the curtains still have an odor. Even the venetian blinds still have it. The television screen has it. So you breathe in this perfumed residue of the smoke into your lungs and immediately the cilia stick out to protect the air sacs. They begin to wash the walls of the lungs like thousands of little windshield wipers. And I can darn near hear myself breathing again and not liking where I am.

Now, I can hear you, the reader who smokes, saying to yourself:

Oh, Jesus, I can't take this. I can't take this holier-than-thou, unsmokier-than-thou attitude.

I empathize with you. I feel your pain. Even

though you know you should quit you don't want someone telling you that you should quit. So maybe you should skip to the next chapter because now I'm going to write about people trying to quit smoking.

So anyway, smokers all want to quit. But they have a problem, which is best described by the old joke where a guy says he knows he can quit smoking because he's done it a hundred times. And I *do* know people who have had their "last" cigarette a hundred times. And each time there's a justification. In other words, they vow to quit after they smoke the "last" cigarette. But then there's another "last" cigarette.

Even though I said I was quitting this morning and said I had my last cigarette with my coffee, I had a rough day today so I will *quit right now, after I have had my "last" cigarette.*

When someone does actually quit, I think there often are two people who quit: the smoker, and the nonsmoking person (or people) who lives with the smoker who quit. (Or maybe the nonsmoker broke up with the smoking person.) Either way, smoke is no longer part of the environment.

If you live with somebody who's a consistent

smoker, you are a smoker also and don't realize it. Because you're living in the apartment, you smell too, but since you're exposed to it every day, it gets to be that you don't notice it as much. So what happens when you break up with that person and you go live in an atmosphere of your own where there's no smoking? You become even more sensitive to the fact that there are people smoking around you and they smell like it.

On the other hand, there have been some people I've run into when I was smoking cigars who would say:

"Gee, that smells good. I love the smell of that. My father was a cigar smoker, and I miss him."

I've also run into cigarette smokers who have quit who go over to where people are smoking— and these nonsmokers may be eight to nine years removed from puffing and inhaling—and say:

"Please don't put that out. I still love the smell of it."

So I don't know what that is. I guess that's a special kind of person. But then there are others who say: "I never want to be there again." And especially someone who just recently quit.

There's this friend of mine who quit smoking. She told me she was going to stop thirty days before her birthday. That was the date. She had set a special day when she was going to quit, and she told me very proudly:

"I'm going to quit smoking thirty days from my birthday."

And I believed her because she has quit a number of times. So I asked her: "Why wait?" And all of a sudden we became combatants.

"Well, why can't I smoke until then?" she demanded, then added with resolve, "I have to do it gradually, I can't just stop right now."

"Why not?" I wondered.

And then she attacked me with:

"It's easy for you. You weren't really smoking. So how can you tell me about smoking when you weren't really smoking, you had a cigar and so you never really inhaled. It's not the same thing."

"You're absolutely correct," I said. "I'm sorry, I just couldn't inhale a cigar. If I did I would have flown out of the room backward."

So we argued for a while. She told me about an article in the paper the other day reporting that the oldest man in America had died, in Louisiana some-where. He was a hundred and three. And the rela-tives said that he was concerned about his health when he got to be ninety-seven, so he quit smoking cigarettes. He'd been smoking them every day since he was about fourteen, but he quit smoking at ninety-seven. And she tried to use this as an exam-ple of how she didn't have to quit smoking right away and smoking doesn't really hurt you if some-body can still be smoking at ninety-seven. But then, using basic mathematics and logic, I said:

"Since he quit smoking at ninety-seven and lived to be a hundred and three, then it seems clear to me that by quitting smoking he must have extended his life for six years."

And so after I gave her all my little ideas about smoking, she agreed she would try to stop before this thirty-days-prior-to-her-birthday date. What I told her was that cigarettes don't have a brain, they go with anybody, and as far as the cigarette compa-nies go, I've never really been able to get a person sitting there with tubes in their nose, inside an oxy-gen tent, in a wheelchair, to admit that they were there because of smoking, that they were in that condition because of smoking. I've never gotten them to tell me anything like that. But they all agree that they never got a get-well card from any cigarette company. Certainly we can't get anybody in the intensive care unit to tell us whether or not they got any postcards. Or even a free carton of cigarettes from the cigarette companies, because the cigarette companies feel that once you're sitting in that position, you no longer have to pay. All you need is that green oxygen tank and the thing stuck in your nose to get a free carton of cigarettes. Or a T-shirt that says: *I'm still smoking*. Or even a hat with the words across the front: *Don't give up. Don't ever give up.*

How hard is it to quit smoking? Well, I saw this thing the other day in a restaurant, a woman had it, and when she pulled it out of her purse it looked like some kind of drug paraphernalia. She was sitting at the next table having a glass of wine. She goes into her purse and pulls out this thing that looks like a cigarette holder, this little thing like the end of a pipe, and she takes it out and she twists it and starts puffing on it. She didn't light it—it's only a little plastic thing—she just twisted it somehow and then put it in her mouth. I was curious, so I leaned over and asked her:

"What is that?"

"It's a nicotine inhaler," she said. "I'm quitting smoking."

I looked at her puffing on that thing, and thought: *I don't know which is worse, smoking a cigarette or sucking on that little plastic thing looking like a drug addict.* But then I thought: *Well at least she's keeping it to herself. She's not bothering anyone else.*

And that's a good thing. Because there are people who decide to smoke those little itty "Bidy" cigarettes that look like a marijuana joint. I'm sure you've seen them. Certainly you've met a lot of these young people who have those cigarettes, and the wonderful explanation they give for smoking these things or for smoking tobacco-less clove cigarettes, is that there's no nicotine. *Okay. But you're still stinking.* And I think these little cigarettes or clove cigarettes or whatever have one of the worst odors on earth. It smells like the young people are lighting up something that was in the vacuum bag.

Having said all this, I must say I feel sorry for today's smoker. Knowing that you have to go into someplace where they won't let you smoke. You have to flick off the lit end of the cigarette and put the other part in your pocket. And so you burn holes in your clothes because you still had a little something burning. I mean, in the old days people who smoked *enjoyed* smoking. They were able to light up anywhere except maybe church—you couldn't light up in church during the sermon—and libraries. But the places where you couldn't smoke were few and far between. I remember people being able to smoke in restaurants. I remember that cigar smoking was accepted, cigarette smoking was accepted. Hollywood stars would have pictures taken, publicity shots, and the cool thing was for them to be holding a cigarette, with smoke going up from the end. Male *and* female. Women did as much to sell cigarettes as did men. Especially in the movies of the 1930s and 1940s.

I remember seeing cigarettes being put out in mashed potatoes. They seemed to make a great putter-outer for a cigarette. You'd be at dinner somewhere and see a cigarette sticking straight up out of a pile of mashed potatoes. And not many people gagged about it. Nobody really ever said: "Oh, that's terrible." I remember people really enjoying smoking, comfortably smoking. When I was in the navy, I saw guys smoking a cigarette while they showered.

I remember a great sign over a urinal:

Please do not throw cigarette butts into the urinal. It makes them soggy and hard to light.

I remember being in a car in the wintertime. Five people in the car and everyone lighting up cigarettes. Nobody rolling down the window, no ventilation, but nobody complaining. A lot of people coughing, but nobody complaining. Lot of eyes watering, but nobody complaining.

In those days when smoking was comfortable, people set beds on fire, falling asleep smoking.

How did the fire happen?

Someone fell asleep with a cigarette. They were trying to smoke in their sleep.

It's a bit nostalgic, really, thinking of those days when smoking was accepted to the point where two people could sit no more than three feet away from each other and smoke in each other's face. I'm talking about smoking, not blowing smoke in the face in terms of "I don't like you," but just talking and smoking, and the smoke would hit the person's face and bounce and swirl up into the person's hair, and nobody said anything. It was just accepted. They sat very relaxed, cigarette in front of the face, elbow on the table, smoke going up into the air, puffing and blowing it out, just very relaxed. People had cigarettes dangling out of their mouths while they picked up a baby. Mothers were holding a baby with a cigarette on the corner of the mouth away from the baby. Ashes dropping on the heads of little children.

Yes. Those were the good old days. Your fingertips tobacco brown from holding and smoking cigarettes. Fingernails brown where you held them, smoke staining your teeth. But now? It's a nightmare. Even in places where you're allowed to smoke you have to ask. And smokers do have very good manners. They will ask politely: "Anyone mind if I smoke?"

Once it is agreed that the smoker can smoke, the smoker reaches into the pack, pulls out the cigarette, turns away from the other people sitting at the table, lights the cigarette, pulls the head back away from the people, takes the arm of the hand holding the cigarette, moves it away from the body in a backward motion, and holds the lips so that smoke blows out of the far corner of the mouth away from the people while the free hand brushes the smoke away from the people. This position makes the smoker look like some kind of deformed person, so I don't see how that person can enjoy smoking. I guess positioning is not everything. For some smokers it is just a matter of getting the nicotine into themselves.

And what about all the taxes being put on the poor cigarette smoker. Seven dollars a pack? That's a great deal of money. If the price of a pack of cigarettes gets any higher, smokers won't have any money left over for their chemotherapy.

It's sad, really, what the smoker has to go through today. It's enough to drive someone to drink. And now, for the first time ever, I'm going to tell you how much alcohol I have consumed during my life. It's a sad story. So be prepared.

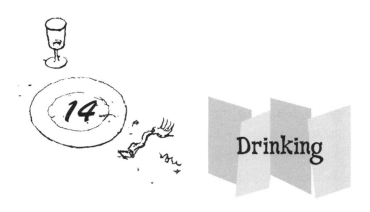

Drinking

How much alcohol have I consumed? I will tell you that you can take the amount of alcohol I have consumed during my lifetime and have the worst party for one person ever. See, I have never been a drinker. I would always rather have had a chili dog or a piece of chocolate cake than a glass of wine or liquor.

I think that the best "don't drink" movie I've ever seen is not *The Lost Weekend* with Ray Milland, who won an Academy Award, or *The Days of Wine and Roses* with Jack Lemmon. I don't know if Jack won an Academy Award or not, but if he didn't he should have. Anyway, those movies didn't really make me feel, gee whiz, you could quit drinking. The movie that made me see alcohol as a horrible problem was *Moulin Rouge*. That little man Toulouse-Lautrec, drinking and drinking and drinking. To see him as a brilliant artist and then to see the women around him who also had drinking problems, it was just too much. And all of the drinking people were loud but made no sense. And I often thought looking at that movie: *Wow! That's what booze does to you!* Somehow when you drink, after a certain amount, your hearing must go out because people who drink a lot become louder when they talk. The reason they become louder, I would assume, is that they don't think they're being heard.

Another way drinking too much affects your ears has to do with balance. Now, we all know that the inner ear is what keeps us standing up. (Certainly, your sense of balance doesn't make a noise unless you fall and take about four tables and a chair out with you and the glasses crash. Then you make a noise.)

Anyway, when you're talking with people who

are drinking, you will notice that most of them, when they've gone to a certain limit with themselves, are just very loud. At some point, after more drinking, at whatever time of night it is, they go from being loud to inaudible and then they become subdued and just mumble. They slur their words. And they must think they're making sense because they laugh at their own jokes.

But there's a certain point early on in their highness where they're very, very loud. And I think it's very difficult to get them to understand that they have to lower their voices. When you try to explain to them that they're too loud, they look at you very strangely and yell:

What do you mean I'm too loud?

And I guess they must say to themselves: *I can't hear myself.* Because everything they say at that point keeps creeping up in volume until they reach about four hundred decibels or whatever.

One of the most amazing things about addiction is how you start out clean, then you become semi-clean, and then you wind up abusing your body by submerging and dousing yourself with whatever it is that you find addictive. And how you start on something often has to do with your so-called friends. For example. There you are. You're clean. You're young. You're in high school. And your friends—they could be all girls or all boys—invite you to a party. Now, for some reason, your brain tells you that in order to prove yourself to these people, you have to take whatever they give you—they've poured something into a giant glass or a silver trophy—and you have to chugalug it while they all say:

"Chugalug, chugalug."

So pretty soon high school ends and after a lot of chugalugs maybe you're semiclean at this point. You've lost a few million brain cells, but you're still more or less semiclean. Now, as a youthful person, you go away to college and start doing things free from the "mismanagement" of parents. You've gone from probably the first freedom you ever had while living with these dictators—which was your room—to *total* freedom.

Speaking of your own room when you lived with your parents, if you have very, very groovy parents, you could set a rule where they have to knock before they enter your room. These are great parents to

Drinking

have. I never had parents like that. My parents had
the idea that because they were paying for things,
since I was not contributing financially, I was somehow their property. I was like the goldfish. So when
the door to my bedroom was closed, they would open
it and say:

"Why is this door closed?"

And I would say something like:

"Because I'm looking in my closet. And the
only way I can open my closet door is to close the
bedroom door."

I never really saw them as spies or anything,
but it was just accepted that they were parents and
because they were parents (even though I never felt
they thought I was in there doing something
wrong), their rule was that the door could never
really be closed. And certainly when I was two,
three, four, five, six, seven years old, I know I didn't
want to close it at night. I wanted it open so they
could come in and save me or I could climb out of
there fast.

But today, some of the parents are just wonderful people and they knock, and the child says:

"Who is it?"

"It's your parents."

"Can you come back later?"

"Oh, yes."

And young people today don't do that much in terms of maintenance. I don't know many young people who do their own laundry, fold the clothes, and put them in the drawer. Sometimes they clean up their room. But there's always been this sort of strange relationship where the kid gets paid to do this, gets an allowance for cleaning the room. This is why I believe so many kids have a problem making an adjustment and why they don't read the paper or think about politics. How can you? You don't want to be responsible for anything. Plus, you're being taught that as long as you're a kid you can be paid to clean up your room. You can be paid to put everything in a neat drawer. You can get an allowance for studying to become something that's going to benefit you in the long run of your life.

But I digress. We were talking about drinking.

So you decide you want to go away to college, and the reasoning is obvious. You want to be able to drink. Smoke cigarettes. Smoke a joint.

Speaking of joint smoking, it is my belief that

marijuana alone does not make you high or alter your thinking. I have watched the behavior of people smoking joints, and it is my belief that by sucking on the smoke, filling your lungs with it, and then not breathing for two to three minutes, you get into oxygen debt on your own. You think it's the marijuana that's doing it but it isn't. When you watch people smoke, and they keep sucking, sucking, and they want to hold the smoke in but the lungs keep pushing, pushing, and then you hear them spurt out, make this sound, and then they try to suck it back in. Between that kind of thing and being bent over, they look like someone just blew skunk smell perfume in their faces. They're sitting with their faces screwed up, trying to hold in the smoke. Then their lungs start panicking and all the organs in the body start reacting:

"Oh, my God! We're going to die!"

And their bodies are now fighting them because all the organs are trying to stay alive, and they scream at the lungs:

"Do something that will keep us alive!"

But still these joint smokers try to hold in the smoke. And they take another drag. They pull hard on the joint, but the joint is a very small thing. So you would imagine that they're getting some oxygen or something that comes with it. But they're trying not to spoil the smoke with oxygen. They fill themselves up again, press the bottom jaw so that the mouth is closed, press their hand against their chest, put their chin on their chest to hold everything down, get that strange look again, like somebody blew skunk fumes in their face, and then they tighten. After about four or five of these exercises with their lungs telling them that at least they want to live, even if the person doesn't, a little bit of smoke sneaks out. And they make these sounds, pulling it back in, and the lungs are scrambling for at least some form of oxygen.

Well, after about six minutes of that, you're going to get dizzy. And I would just like to suggest that one time, as an experiment, someone try all of the above maneuvers without a joint in their hand. I would imagine that going through the exercise of smoking a joint for six minutes—even without the effect of marijuana—I bet you you'll get a high from it.

So, you'll be able to smoke on a college campus. You'll be able to smoke a joint. Some of you have never smoked, but once you get to college, you'll meet friends—quote-unquote friends—who will teach you how to smoke. They will tell you you're nobody unless you've had a joint. Now these are very knowledgeable people who will tell you why a joint is good for you. And there's always the wonderful story of the person who smokes a joint and didn't feel high and didn't understand what the big deal was all about but wound up eating sofa covers with salt and ketchup on it.

Anyway, back to drinking. There are many, many teenagers who, by the time they get to college, are already pros at consuming beer and all other permutations of alcohol. But it's that thing of getting along that makes you step up the pace of drinking at college when there are no parents to come in your room. So the sense of belonging cheers you on. Someone says in so many words:

"You will be my friend. You'll be friends of the fraternity, the sorority, the club."

So you feel you belong if you chugalug and they sing "Chugalug, chugalug" and you down this drink made from eight different alcoholic beverages.

Gin. Bourbon. Whatever. Something halfway sweet so it's a little smoother. And after that, what happens? You become sick. And you go to the bathroom and you throw up and your friends are laughing at you. So you chugalug for these people who are your friends and you become very sick and you wind up with your face in a toilet. So much for friendship.

That's the thing about drinking. It's very gradual. And even after you are someone who some people might call an alcoholic, you still do it gradually. One day, for example, I spent the afternoon at a friend's house. He and his wife and I were watching a football game when he said to his wife:

"Honey, how about a screwdriver?"

And so his wife went to the bar they had in the corner of the living room and mixed some vodka into a glass of orange juice. Well, they had about five of these screwdrivers—and I saw her making them a little stronger each time—until finally he said:

"Honey, forget the orange juice."

And, of course, there comes a time when some people realize they are drinking too much and they want to cut back. So sometimes they set a time when they can start drinking. Let's say five o'clock. They have decided that they will not have a drink until five o'clock. Which is good. But then they start looking at their watch around noon, and by three o'clock they are just sitting in a chair, holding on to the arms of the chair, and staring at their watch.

What about moderation? I asked my friend that day—the one who started with the vodka and orange juice and finished with just vodka:

"Why can't you drink in moderation?"

And he asked me:

"Why can't you *eat* in moderation?"

So I thought about the concept of moderation. As I said before, doctors love this word. They say:

"You can do such and such."

And then they add:

"In *moderation*."

And so I decided I should address the idea of moderation. What do I know about moderation? Let me tell you.

Moderation

If the Shoe Fits

The mind, your own mind, my own mind, is an amazing thing. And one of the most amazing things is how you can talk yourself into almost anything. Eating. Smoking. Drinking. You can rationalize all of these things. Which is why the mere thought of moderation is doomed from the beginning. The mind kills the thought immediately.

The problem is, people won't admit that they are talking themselves into things. That's how good the mind can be when it comes to fooling the body. So, in an attempt to figure out how the mind works, I began to look at things that could offer proof of how the mind tricks you. And I don't mean proof that takes years to show up. I mean *instant* proof. Like when you buy a pair of shoes that you know are too tight but you buy them anyway.

Women are not the only ones who buy shoes that are too narrow, too short, and that pinch. A man will see a loafer or some lace-up shoe that is absolutely fantastic and try it on and even walk around in the store wearing it. And maybe it feels too tight. So he will say to the salesman:

"Do you have this in a ten and a half?"

And the salesman will say no. And the person will say:

"Well, I can make these fit. Okay. I'll take these."

What no one ever realizes is how much heat is generated—as you move—between that leather, the sock, and your skin. And I've seen men— grown men—start out walking like they are on a military march—looking very fresh, as if they are marching off for chow—and then after a few steps turn into someone who is bent over, looking like they have done nine miles in the desert with no water. Their feet are just killing them. And the blisters. And they just continue to walk. They won't take them off. Just continue to walk. And finally there's that night after wearing these shoes all day. And they take them off. Take off the shoe and the sock and they look. And there's all that skin pulled back. And some blisters. And all anyone can say to themselves at that point is:

"I told myself that it wasn't going to hurt, that these shoes were okay."

And you try to make the adjustment, but it's just stupid. You've talked yourself into something that you're going to pay for. Because you want it. You want to look cool.

You do the same with a shirt. More than once I've had a shirt—a favorite shirt that I really liked—and I've given great pain to my thumbs trying to button the top button of the shirt, when, in fact, the collar was too tight. And I would find myself making about twenty passes at getting that button through the hole—knowing that it was too tight—trying not to rip the button off. Because I've got to put the tie on. And then to see one's own skin doubled over, covering up the collar, because you've pulled so hard on the skin on the neck. And you start to talk and you sound like Arnold Stang.

And then there are the pants you put on and you keep pulling and sucking in until you can button that button. And the fat rolls over it, and embarrassingly the button part of your pants folds over also, so that the white of your pants is showing and indicating to everybody that your pants are very much too tight.

And what about the zipper? You zip it and it goes zigzag instead of straight up. So now you have forced on a pair of pants that you know are so tight that you can't sit down because if you do you're going to hear @#!*% in the center. There's no room for the fabric to expand, and so it rips.

I remember going someplace, putting on a jacket I liked, a jacket that said CENTRAL HIGH SCHOOL. I was fifteen. It was January in Philadelphia, Pennsylvania. The temperature, thirty-six degrees. I have a shirt, sweater, and this cotton Central High School jacket. And I'm going to go over to this girl's house. She's cute. So I'm going to risk catching pneumonia for her. That's how cute she is. (Which is, of course, the same logic that one uses when risking heart disease by eating bad fats.)

I close the door to my house and I don't have a car so I'm going to take the bus. It's about seven in the evening. Thirty-six degrees. And the breeze hits my face, but I just left my house. And I checked myself. I said:

Are you going to be able to negotiate this?

And I answered myself.

Yeah, it's not that *cold, everything is cool, everything is fine.*

And I walk two blocks to the bus stop. I still have some of the warmth of my own house with me, and the bus comes within five minutes. The breeze hits me again and I get a little shake, but nothing to worry about, because I've got my cool Central High School jacket on. The bus was warm, there were about nine people on it, and I rode over to her house. I got off at the corner, walked to her house, knocked on the door. She answered. Her parents were there. And I had on my Central High School jacket. She thought I was cool. Her parents loved me too because I was wearing my Central High School jacket.

Now, it wasn't a leather jacket, it was just a cotton jacket, which is not a January jacket, but it said Central High School. I hated to take it off. But we were inside, so I took off my jacket and we sat on the couch until we finally waited out her parents. Either we waited them out or the parents were very nice and they went upstairs and we went into the kitchen to pretend we were going to study and we did some macking, that's kissing, no fondling. Just kissing. Attempts were made by me, but she was like an Olympic boxing referee and she stopped me.

Stop!

And I'd stop. Then we would go back to kissing. I'd make another move.

Stop!

A little warning. And it was I guess maybe around eleven when the final voice came down from upstairs.

Myrtle!

Myrtle Boxcar. She was, I think, pretty close to one of the last Myrtles ever. The name Myrtle is very difficult to find these days. I think there's one up in Saskatoon and another in Rangoon. Myrtle Witherspoon in Rangoon. And I've often wondered whatever happens to thirty-five-year-old women named Bambi. The name Bambi just kind of falls off after that, I don't know what name they take on or if there's a report at city hall on how many Bambis changed their name. I guess the records would say something like: Bambi Ranovskovburn has changed her first name to Helen. Myrtle, by the way, and I'm not going to digress about names much more, but Myrtle is a name you can't shorten. Myrt? Not good. Sounds like you've been cut off in the middle of what you were saying.

So anyway, as I was saying, this voice came down from upstairs.

Myrtle!

The voice had the kind of tone that made you not want to see what they were going to say next. So I left her house. I put on my Central High School cotton jacket and walked outside. Right away I realized that the temperature had dropped. I heard the door lock behind and a wind came. It had been blowing already. I just stepped into it. This wind was about nine miles an hour, but it was consistent. In those days I didn't know anything about windchill. I just knew that somebody took the thirty-six and turned it into a twenty in just the amount of time I was at Myrtle's house. And that cotton jacket was a sieve. It just allowed whatever wanted to come in to come in.

I went to the corner and I'm telling you I was still hot from those kisses and holding her and my hormones were flowing. And the wind went into the corduroy pants. It entered at twenty degrees. Muscles started to shiver up the back, the chest, the neck. I started to vibrate. I went into turbulence. It was my body trying to keep me warm.

I stood on the corner shaking, but there was no sign of a bus. Suddenly, I did not feel cool and smooth in that cotton jacket. I tried to seek shelter, but the wind followed me everywhere I went. I stood in the doorway of a store, waiting for the bus, and my nose began to run and my eyes began to run and I thought:

Why would one's nose run? What was my nose trying to do? What was my body trying to tell me?

And then my jaw muscles went into turbulence. My whole face was shaking. My neck was shaking. That's how cold it was. My neck was vibrating. I had to keep my mouth partially open to keep my teeth from cracking. My teeth were going up and down; they wanted to rattle. And I think I stood there for eighteen minutes. At least eighteen minutes. Since temperatures have a windchill factor, I will factor eighteen minutes of standing in a windchill of sixteen degrees (the temperature was falling fast), so I calculated that eighteen minutes in a sixteen-degree temperature with a cotton jacket from Central High School is equal to two hours in a blizzard.

Finally, the bus came. I was so happy to see it. Unfortunately, my muscles were so stiff that when the guy opened the door, I just fell into the bus. When I hit the steps of the bus, I thought I was going to be like a candy cane. Yes, I was so cold I thought I was going to shatter. My hand would wind up under the driver's seat, a piece of my elbow would be on the steps. My head would roll off and be between some woman's shoes. And everything just hurt. It just hurt.

The bus driver got up and helped me into the bus. Then he started to drive and the worst thing happened. I sat down and reached into my pocket to get the money for the fare. I searched for the money, dug my hand deep into my pocket, but there was nothing there.

In those days, I think the fare might have been something like twenty cents. But I didn't have a penny, even though I knew when I left my house I had twenty cents bus fare. Then, of course, I realized what must have happened. While this girl and I were wrestling around on the floor, kissing and making each other's temperature go up and down, I think the twenty cents must have fallen out of my pocket. So I must have left the twenty cents in her house. Which did me no good on the bus.

I looked at that bus driver and said: "Mister, I've lost the twenty cents. Please don't put me off."

I guess he felt sorry for me because he let me ride all the way to the corner down the street from my house. I got off and I walked. I think I did one block before the wind came back again. It was blowing. It was howling. It was horrible.

My eyes were watering as I headed into the last block. And I started to run toward my house. I think I ran about seven steps before my brain started yelling at me:

Stop! Stop! Don't you realize how stupid this is? By running, you are increasing the windchill factor!

So I tried to walk backward and that wasn't helping either, because the wind was swirling and the back was just as cold as the front. I tried to go sideways. I tried to skip sideways, I tried to run backward. Finally I got to the front of my house. There were no cars. Nobody. Nothing out there. I walked up to the door of my house, and as I reached into my pocket, I remembered that while I was looking for my twenty cents I hadn't found a key. Obviously, I had left my key on the floor while Myrtle and I were rolling around making each other get hot and cold.

I thought about staying outside all night, but it was too cold. See, I didn't want to ring the doorbell because these people I lived with both worked and it was late. So I knew if I rang the doorbell I would wake them up. But it was either freeze to death or wake up these people, so I rang the doorbell.

The light came on in the hallway and my father opened the door. He was dressed in his boxer shorts—he was in the navy—and a white T-shirt. My father weighed 230 pounds. And he opened the door, no slippers, and he looked at me, obviously upset because I woke him up or I woke up my mother and she woke him up, that's probably what happened, and she said go down and open the door.

I stepped inside the vestibule. He closed the door, looked at me, and asked:

"Where's your key?"

And I said:

"I don't know. I lost it. *And* I lost my bus fare."

My father frowned and said:

"How did you do that?"

He was upset because he had to open the door and so he wanted to know exactly how it had happened.

"I lost my key over at Myrtle's house," I said.

My father pressed for a more complete explanation.

"How did you lose it over there?"

"I don't know."

My father looked at me, well not at me, at my jacket. And he said:

"How come you're wearing this? What are you doing with this cotton jacket on?"

I said: "Well, I just put it on."

He said: "Do you know what the temperature is outside?"

And I looked at him like he had lost his mind. I said:

"I just came in from outside."

He said: "Yeah, but you don't act like it. You act like you think this is June or something. You want to catch your death of cold?"

My father was very smart and he knew the real reason I had on a cotton jacket in January. He frowned and said:

"Couldn't you just tell people you went to Central High School? What the hell you've got to wear a cotton jacket for?"

"Well," I said, "I just went over to Myrtle's house."

My father thought for a moment and then did what he usually did: He repeated the facts of the situation. He said:

"You wore that cotton jacket? And you didn't have bus fare?"

"Well," I said. "I thought I had it, but I lost it."

My father was incredulous. "You're out there freezing to death, trying to impress this girl?"

"Yeah," I said. "I guess so."

"And," my father asked, "you heard the door lock close behind you at Myrtle's place?"

"Yeah," I said.

"And you were just so in love," my father said. "*So* in love."

"Yeah," I said.

My father loved it. He laughed and said:

"How cold were you?"

"I was shivering."

My father laughed again and said:

"All because of this cotton jacket? All because you were trying to impress a girl?"

"Yeah," I said.

"And you fell down in the bus?"

"Yeah," I said.

My father chuckled and said:

"You've got to get a dog. You need a friend. You don't need a girlfriend who's going to put you out of the house, keep your money, and lock the door. Get a dog. You don't have to impress the dog; the dog will appreciate you no matter what high school you go to, just as long as you take it out and then come back.

"You've got to get a dog. Then you don't have to leave the house. Just sleep with the dog."

And that was his joke. He loved it. As long as he lived, he would once in a while look at me, no matter how old I got, and he would remember that night coming from Myrtle's house. And he would laugh and say:

"You've got to get a dog."

Every holiday, he would laugh and say:

"You've got to get a dog."

I miss spending holidays with my father. *And*, I'm almost ashamed to say, I miss the food. Because on holidays you can eat like a pig and tell yourself: *But it's a holiday*.

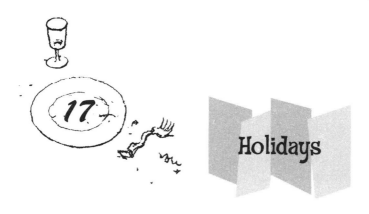

Holidays

Holidays are wonderful. It doesn't matter which holiday, any holiday is just fantastic. Thanksgiving? Fantastic. Christmas? Fantastic. George Washington's Birthday? Roll out the cherry pie! In other words, holidays have a built-in rationale for eating. You *have* to eat on a holiday. Why else did they make holidays except to eat?

Holidays bring out the women who cook once a year. I mean, some women, of course, cook every day. These everyday cookers are there on holidays too. But the women who cook once a year (because it's a holiday) are the scariest of all. They have waited all year to make what they call "their specialty." And their specialty never is something healthy. And why should it be? It's a holiday!

Women who cook once a year. Only. Once a year. They cook something and bring it. One by one they file in like gastronomic grim reapers bearing death in a casserole dish. Which is why holiday tables are so bad for you. Especially Thanksgiving. There are so many starches in one place. Potato salad. Candied yams. Stuffing. Rice. All these are Aunt Somebody's favorite. So you have dueling candied yams. A lot of women bring candied yams. Sometimes with marshmallows on top. Glazed broccoli. Bread. In fact, several kinds of bread. Depending on your region—the region where you live—you can have as many as six different kinds of bread. Corn bread. Biscuits. Sourdough rolls. Soda bread. Olive loaf. Zucchini bread. Rolls. Doesn't make any difference. It's still bread. Starch. Carbohydrates.

And then you get to the turkey. Somebody brought a deep-fried turkey and somebody else brought an oven-roasted turkey. And the whole idea is to eat until your stomach muscles begin to stretch so much that your stomach is distended and you just feel horrible. And your body goes to work in a desperate attempt to digest all this food. But before your stomach can digest even the stuff you ate before the turkey, you've got all these desserts. And the funny thing about desserts is that many times they duplicate what you had for the main course. You have to try the sweet potato pie, duplicating the candied yams you had and the sweet potato stuffing. Then you have rice pudding, which duplicates the wild rice you already had too much of. Bread pudding, which duplicates all the breads that you had. Cheesecake, which duplicates your cheese.

But it doesn't end there. The day after Thanksgiving you're doing leftovers. You're taking eggs and scrambling them with sweet potatoes and so forth and so on. Then you're having turkey sandwiches for a week. And, of course, you're still eating the bread. Finally it gets down to turkey soup.

Holidays. All about eating. Easter? You have Easter *eggs*. Even birthdays, which are really personal holidays. What do you have? Birthday *cake*. So the best thing to do is avoid all holidays. (On the other hand, you *could* say that holidays only come along "once in a while." And didn't the doctor say "once in a while" was okay?)

Another thing about holidays is that when family and friends get together, you get caught up on all the news. And sometimes you get bad news. And the next thing you know, you're going to a funeral.

The Bitter End

When someone is laid out in what I call "the permanent horizontal parade rest," his family and friends are, of course, very sad. So they have a funeral. In fact, I was at a funeral the other day and I ran into a friend of mine who is seventy-seven years old. I hadn't seen him in a very long time. Years had gone by. As he was walking towards me, I saw that he was walking slowly. And it's the first time I'd ever seen him walking with a cane. And I thought to myself, "Wow. I hope it's not bad."

I put an arm around him and gave him a good squeeze and then stepped back and looked at him.

His eyes reminded me of those of a goldfish in a bowl, a goldfish that's almost belly up but not quite. Just floating mostly. His eyes were all misty and everything.

"How you feeling, man?" I asked my friend.

I posed the question in that way you do when you don't really expect them to tell you all the details. And this man, this old friend of mine, with the cane in his hand, and that goldfish look in his eyes, looked up at me and said: "All I know is, I'm on *this* side of the grass."

Anyway, after a funeral they always have a get-together afterward at someone's house and the people who miss their friend or family member cry. They also reminisce about the dearly departed. Their life. Their personality. Their work. And, unless this person died of old age at 106, the people at the funeral or gatherings will eventually get around to discussing why they died at whatever age they died.

I have been to funerals and memorials during my life, and although they are solemn occasions worthy of reflection, the behavior of some of the people in attendance would seem to be bizarre in any other given situation. For example, if a group of people were standing at the scene of a car accident on an icy road and someone said, "The car went off the road because of the ice," when people got back in their own cars they would drive very, very carefully as they continued down the road. Not so at funerals.

I remember attending one funeral where the guy was like the poster boy for not smoking. Everyone knew he was a heavy smoker and he didn't take care of himself. So at a young age, this guy died of smoking-related illness. He had all the diseases. Everything. And he had spent the last months of his life with tubes in his mouth. Outside the church, in the parking lot, a group of his friends stopped to lament the loss. The conversation went something like this:

"I told him to stop smoking," one friend said.

"Yes," answered another friend. "He should have stopped."

"He was really addicted," another friend said, shaking her head.

Now all this would have been fine except for the fact that the people saying these things were *smoking* as they talked. I mean, their friend is in a closed coffin and they know he died of smoking but here they are, smoking themselves.

In fact, it's the same at all funerals regardless of the reason someone has died. I have been to funerals for people who died of severely clogged arteries that led to heart failure, and then gone to a wake where they served fried chicken, fried potatoes, chocolate cake, cheesecake, ice cream, and everything they could find that was full of saturated and trans-fats.

"I hear he had cholesterol of nine hundred and fifty," someone said as he stuffed a piece of coconut pie in his face.

"He should have taken better care of himself," another person commiserated as she spread butter on a dinner roll.

And then there was another time when someone died of cirrhosis brought on by extremely heavy drinking. At a reception after the funeral what did his friends do?

"Here's to John," one of his friends said as he raised a glass of whiskey.

"Here, here," his friends and family answered in unison, all of them raising their own glass.

And then, as they were drinking, someone in the group actually said:

"I told him not to drink."

And everybody nodded as they downed whatever they had in their glasses.

Maybe it's the grief. Maybe they don't think it can happen to them. Whatever it is, one can see that even at a funeral people still don't get it. They arrive in a long line of cars that goes very slowly so they have plenty of time to think about the situation. They know why their friend or family member died. They *know*. But then they do the same thing that caused this person to die.

And once again, I'm not pointing fingers. At the funeral for the guy who died of overplaquing and severe amounts of clogging cholesterol, I was too busy licking chocolate icing off my fingers to point one.

The Unkindest Cut

In all the years of living with this body, I don't think that I have ever finished cutting my toenails without going too deep, too far, or pulling out some root corner, or tender side, of a nail. And sometimes even drawing a little blood. Not too much, but enough so that when you put on a sock and a shoe and begin to walk you realize what toe exists on that particular foot.

After some sixty-five years—or at least counting thirty-nine of the sixty-five years, which is the time I have been married and have been *forced* to cut my nails—I still cannot properly cut the nail of a toe. And many times it's not the whole foot that I manage to mangle, it's just one toe. And not always the same one.

They have invented many wonderful devices to perform this task. However, no matter which device I use, I still harm myself.

This reminds me of the fact that I am what I ate and I'm afraid. Because I now notice that my nails are more brittle than they were when I was young. Even my nails are old parts now. And I now realize —I knew it all the time but I never kept it in focus— that I should have eaten more protein and fruits and vegetables. These are the things in a diet that keep nails healthy. But now my nails are made of hot dogs, hoagies, bacon, chocolate, and all those things I ate. I let my nails down. I failed them. And I read somewhere that the only thing I can do to help them now is to soak them in olive oil for thirty minutes a day. Thirty minutes a day! That's what I'm faced with. I didn't eat enough vegetables, so now I have to act like one. To sit there with my feet in a bowl of olive oil like some big piece of celery dipping itself.

And although I may never learn how to cut my toenails in a way that does not harm myself, I have finally figured out how to eat and not harm myself. I have finally realized that exercise is good. That smoking is bad. And now I am attempting to live a healthy lifestyle. But it is quite an effort. So I will tell you that I promise to keep away from bad foods unless I have a good excuse. Even then I will eat bad foods only once in a while. Which makes me wonder when I last had a piece of anything bad for me. Maybe I can have something bad now. Let me think. When was it that I had a wonderful piece of fried something or a rich fat-filled dessert?

For the life of me, I can't remember.

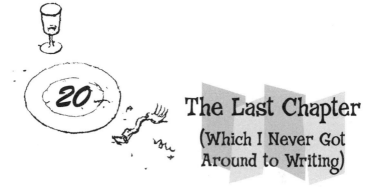

The Last Chapter
(Which I Never Got Around to Writing)

After writing a lot of pages, I began to wonder what it all meant. That's when I realized I had reached the point where the author is supposed to wrap everything up so that the book makes sense. But that's not comedy. Still, I thought I needed to do something. So I broke it down and came up with three choices everyone has:

1. Don't go to the doctor at all. Just ignore everything until one day your eyeballs roll up under your eyebrows, your body slumps forward, and you wake up in traffic in the back of a large, strange vehicle.

2. Pay for doctors, pills, and machinery.

3. Stay healthy.

Obviously it is much cheaper and far more intelligent if you take care of yourself in terms of health. Why? Because pills cost $400 a month. Machinery even more. And if you have hypertension, diabetes, and high cholesterol, your total bill may be as high as $800 a month. Now, that's a lot of money. Plus, if you go in the hospital, seeing the doctor, that can bring it up to pretty close to around $2,500 a month. Now, you can't afford that. But if you have your health, you can use your Social Security check. Let's say your Social Security check gives you $900 a month. If you're not ill, that's a lot of money.

Unfortunately, that's as far as I got in my summation because I was interrupted by a call from my cousin Winona, Aunt T'Glivea's daughter. It seems that Aunt T'Glivea fell out while watching *Days of Our Lives.* Well, I don't really know if she was watching it but that's what was on television when they found her. Her eyes were closed and she had both legs tangled around a cushion and a telephone cord. Poor Aunt T'Glivea. At times, as of late, she has been known to drift just a shade off the page and maybe into another chapter of another book.

Anyway, seems that cousin Winona called an ambulance. And it was there very fast because it seems this is a neighborhood where they keep them at both ends of the cul de sac. So they take Aunt T'Glivea to the hospital—which is not really her hospital—and a doctor who is not really her doctor examines her. She's diagnosed with a case of "we don't know." Then they see that there's more money left on her insurance card so they run the tests again, this time under the name of MRI.

So by now, Aunt T'Glivea is thoroughly checked into the hospital. They give her IVs. Of course, they don't know why they're giving them to her, but this is cookie-cutter medical practice: Give the person water with sugar in it. Aunt T'Glivea is fine in the daytime. She lets the IV drip and she watches *Days of Our Lives*. But at night . . .

For some reason they put Aunt T'Glivea on the ICU ward. There's a left side and a right side. If you're on the left side it seems that you're not doing well at all. But Aunt T'Glivea is on the other side, where they have no idea what the person is doing or what the disease is. And it's also the side of the ward where the doctors haven't come in yet. By the way, this is a weekend, and by Monday the doctors will not be on strike but they won't be found because they are having an argument with the insurance company. The same insurance company from which they extracted money using Aunt T'Glivea card.

As I was saying—and was reported to me by my cousin Winona—Aunt T'Glivea, for some reason, at night, in the darkness of the hallways, because the hospital is trying to save money by shutting down lights, wanders through the hallway trying to go home. Aunt T'Glivea has set off, in three days, nine alarms.

I was given a phone number to call Aunt T'Glivea and wish her well, which I'm happy to do, because she seems to be very lucid when she's talking to me except that I don't know the people she's talking about. In other words, the stories connect but I don't know the players and she keeps telling me that I know them and I'm getting worried about myself.

So I call Aunt T'Glivea because I am the strong nephew she will listen to. (At least this is what I'm told.) I dial the room number and a woman's voice says hello. And I say:

"Aunt T'Glivea, this is your favorite nephew. How are you?"

The voice said:

"This is not your Aunt T'Glivea and don't call here anymore because I'm sick."

And then whoever it was hung up.

I called my cousin Winona and I said:

"Where is Aunt T'Glivea?"

Winona said: "They moved her but they didn't tell anybody."

So there was Aunt T'Glivea—in the hospital somewhere. When you dial and ask for Aunt T'Glivea they say:

"We don't have any information. Are you a friend of the family?"

This is over the phone where they can't see me. Anybody can say—if you can't see them—anybody can call up and say:

"Yes. I am a friend of the family."

"Okay, we'll put you through."

This makes no sense. But then again, this is a hospital. Their job is to save lives, not make sense.

Cousin Winona finally found Aunt T'Glivea. She's now in the peaceful ward, but she's on the side where they do certain things. On the other side they don't do these certain things. She's on the side where the people, at night, are allowed to wander because the doors don't have the alarms on them.

"How far can the patients go?" I asked cousin Winona.

It seems there's a cinder-block wall that blocks the doors. This was dreamt up by psychiatrists who feel patients have a right to open a door but go nowhere.

I then began to ask questions about Aunt T'Glivea.

"Winona. What did the doctors say about Aunt T'Glivea falling out?"

It seems that Aunt T'Glivea's doctor finally showed up to explain part of the test results. (Although he kept saying that certain tests are out of his expertise.) Can we stop and think for a minute about the old days when a doctor was allowed to say:

"I'm just a hip person. I don't know about the thigh or the ankle or the shin."

Anyway, Aunt T'Glivea's doctor finally says that Aunt T'Glivea is anemic. That's why she fell out. So we feel better. We're breathing better. There's nothing wrong with Aunt T'Glivea, it's just that she's anemic. Why is she anemic? Well, from the blood tests it seems that she's lost three-fourths of her blood. They took blood to find out why she's losing blood. I didn't mean to cause trouble but I asked my cousin:

"Did they put the blood back, after using it for the tests, because she really needs some."

"No," Winona said, "but when she gets better, Aunt T'Glivea owes the hospital four pints of blood."

It seems the doctor began to look at the medication she's taking. And it seems that there are about three or four pills Aunt T'Glivea has to take. There's one pill she takes in the morning and at night and the other two in the afternoon. Now, Aunt T'Glivea is a very intelligent woman. She knows there are times when she will forget. Therefore, to protect against her forgetfulness, Aunt T'Glivea takes both pills in the morning. In other words, she knows that she might forget the evening pill so she takes both pills in the morning, because she can remember that, along with a glass of orange juice. Which means that there's a hole burning in the intestinal track some-where and she's losing blood.

You see, God and nature have a way of telling you that you need to pay attention to something you're doing.

So here I am sitting outside of a wonderful hot dog place watching the young people—*so* young. And a young man, who must be around nineteen or twenty (with his jaws puffed out while chewing, chewing rapidly, swallowing, chewing), is enjoying what has to be a chili dog with sauerkraut. There are three more of them in front of him but one bite remains in his right hand. He has a system. He bites. He closes his mouth. He wipes. He chews. He swallows. He wipes. And then he bites. And then he takes a huge gulp of a dark soda, forcing a turbulence of foam inside the bottle, then lower-ing the bottle from his lips, still chewing as his eyes water, he places the bottle on the table, raises his free hand high above his head, leans to his right, opens his empty mouth and belches. A big, full, clearing belch making room for more, like the settling of a fault. The left hand comes down and picks up three French fries with cheese on them. Cheese and ketchup on them. He bites and shoves. They're gone. And then the wipe. Chewing. Swallowing. And then the empty mouth finishes the remains of the chili dog with sauerkraut that was in the right hand.

Ah, yes, I know the feeling. And I think to myself: He is what he's eating and about forty years from now he's going to be frightened.